S0-AKZ-704

LHC

10/09

Selecting a College Major

Selecting a College Major

Exploration and Decision Making

Sixth Edition

Virginia N. Gordon, Ph.D.
Susan J. Sears, Ph.D.
The Ohio State University

Prentice Hall
Upper Saddle River,
New Jersey Columbus, Ohio

Library of Congress Cataloging-in-Publication Data

Gordon, Virginia N.
    Selecting a college major: exploration and decision making / Virginia N. Gordon, Susan J. Sears.—6th ed.
      p. cm.
    Includes bibliographical references.
    ISBN-13: 978-0-13-715279-7 (pbk.)
    ISBN-10: 0-13-715279-5 (pbk.)
    1. College majors.   I. Sears, Susan Jones.   II. Title.
LB2361.G67 2010
378.2'41—dc22

                                            2008053015

Vice President and Editor in Chief: Jeffery W. Johnston
Executive Editor: Sande Johnson
Editorial Assistant: Lynda Cramer
Senior Managing Editor: Pamela D. Bennett
Project Manager: Kerry J. Rubadue
Production Coordination: Thistle Hill Publishing Services, LLC
Art Director: Candace Rowley
Cover Image: iStockphoto
Cover Design: Diane Ernsberger
Media Project Manager: Rebecca Norsic
Senior Operations Supervisor: Matthew Ottenweller
Operations Specialist: Susan W. Hannahs
Vice President, Director of Sales & Marketing: Quinn Perkson
Senior Marketing Manager: Amy Judd
Marketing Coordinator: Brian Mounts

This book was set in Times by Integra. It was printed and bound by Bind-Rite Graphics/Robbinsville. The cover was printed by Coral Graphics.

Pearson® is a registered trademark of Pearson plc
Merrill® is a registered trademark of Pearson Education, Inc.

Pearson Education Ltd. London
Pearson Education Singapore Pte. Ltd.
Pearson Education Canada, Inc.
Pearson Education–Japan
Pearson Education Australia PTY, Limited

Pearson Education North Asia, Ltd., Hong Kong
Pearson Educación de Mexico, S.A. de C.V.
Pearson Education Malaysia Pte. Ltd.
Pearson Education Upper Saddle River,
  New Jersey

Prentice Hall
is an imprint of

www.pearsonhighered.com

10 9 8 7 6 5 4 3 2 1
ISBN-13: 978-0-13-715279-7
ISBN-10:   0-13-715279-5

Dedication

This book is dedicated to all students who are undecided or want to change a college major and who face the challenge of deciding with fortitude and courage.

Brief Contents

Contents

Unit Four   Exploring Occupations   61

Unit Five   Making a Decision   75

Note: Every effort has been made to provide accurate and current Internet information in this book. However, the Internet and information on it are constantly changing, so it is inevitable that some of the Internet addresses listed in this textbook will change.

Preface

Choosing a college major can be a difficult and sometimes confusing decision for many students. First-year college students, in particular, have little experience with many of the academic disciplines represented in college curricula. They have limited understanding of how knowledge is "artificially" divided into smaller units or disciplines and how the sum of this knowledge is interrelated and intertwined.

Many entering students have only a vague idea of what a "major" entails, not only in the coursework required, but in its real-life applications in the work world. This even includes some community college technical majors. Some students wrongly perceive that their choice of major leads directly to a "job."

With the bewildering array of educational and career options available today, many students choose to be "undecided" when they enter college. They recognize the advantage of exploring the academic options open to them on their campus. This workbook is designed to assist them in this information-gathering and deciding process.

Often students want or need to change the major they initially chose. Some change for personal reasons, such as a lack of interest in the subject matter or exposure to other academic areas that lead to new interests. Some students cannot retain their initial choice of major because of their inability to perform academically at a certain level in the required coursework. This problem, in addition to the limited number of applicants taken into some selective or oversubscribed majors, creates a situation that forces students to choose other majors.

Advanced students who are rethinking an earlier choice might be somewhat constrained by their earned academic credit that may not be viable for some of the alternative majors they are considering. This is especially true of students who want to change to two-year technical majors. Students who are in the process of changing majors need the type of academic advising that can help them integrate previous course credit into new directions. Up until now, there has been no publication to help this large (and sometimes unrecognized or unacknowledged) group of students explore other choices in a systematic way. This workbook has been developed to assist not only the "undecided" student with selecting a major, but also the "major-changer" who is exploring alternative options.

Unit One encourages students to review their current academic situation and helps them assess their method for approaching and making decisions, both past and present. *Unit Two* involves students in self-assessment and helps them consider their personal strengths and limitations. *Unit Three* is concerned with identifying and exploring various academic major options from three perspectives. Students select several realistic majors and collect detailed information about them.

Once these academic areas have been identified, students explore related occupational fields in *Unit Four*. *Unit Five* helps them narrow down alternatives so that appropriate academic planning can take place. Developing an academic graduation plan helps students summarize all they have learned into a practical vehicle for future planning and implementation. *Unit Six* guides students in implementing their academic major decision. The appendix offers an optional opportunity for students who are interested in developing their resume writing and job searching skills.

This workbook leads students through an orderly, rational approach to selecting a college major. Not only are students encouraged to gather detailed educational and career information, but they are also encouraged to identify their feelings about the process as they are experiencing it. The authors hope this combination of cognitive and effective searching will lead to satisfying, long-term, realistic educational decisions.

This new edition reflects the incredible technological advancement of the Internet, which provides the information resources that are so important in educational and occupational decision making. Internet resources include those for assessing one's personal interests, abilities, and values; information about myriad educational options; and (perhaps the most extensive) information resources for exploring occupational fields that have direct or indirect connections to academic areas. Many of the assignments in this workbook require students to access the Internet for this information.

The authors wish to thank George Steele, Melinda McDonald, Tracy Tupman, and Margie Bogenschutz, whose understanding and sensitivity to these types of college students provided many insights into the approaches used in this workbook. For sharing their expertise with us as reviewers of this new edition, special thanks to Maria Annett Day, Norfolk State University; Donna G. Lamb, The Ohio State University–Lima Campus; and Keith Alan Rocci, University of Alabama.

Introduction

*The individual becomes conscious of himself as being this particular
individual with particular gifts, tendencies, impulses, passions, under
the influence of a particular product of his milieu. He who becomes thus
conscious of himself assumes all this as part of his own responsibility.
At the moment of choice he is in complete isolation, for he withdraws from
his surroundings; and he is in complete continuity, for he chooses himself
as product; and this choice is a free choice, so that we might even say,
when he chooses himself as product, that he is producing himself.*

—Søren Kierkegaard

One of the first important decisions you face when you enter college is the choice of
an area of study. Some students are very certain about their choice of college major,
some are tentatively decided but have some doubts, some have narrowed their
options to two or three, and some are totally undecided. Regardless of the decision
level you initially experience, you need some time to either confirm your choice or
explore academic alternatives. The process of confirmation or exploration needs to
involve you in the gathering and integration of information. If you are exploring, you
need to be involved in learning not only about the possible majors at your institution
and what coursework is required, but also about how specific majors relate to your
personal characteristics and career goals.

You may be a student who has found that after you have made a choice of major,
your plans are thwarted. Perhaps your initial choice was not realistic or attainable,
based on your own changing interests or abilities, or the institution's policies about
selective or oversubscribed majors. It is critical for you as a major-changer to examine
your personal strengths in a new light and to identify new majors that will satisfy your
changing academic and career goals. Students often have questions about the role of
majors in their college education. Several of these questions are considered next.

WHAT IS A MAJOR?

A *college major* is a specialized area of study intended to give you a concentration
of knowledge in a particular academic field. The number of courses or credit
hours required in a major (in addition to the general coursework specified by your
institution) will depend on the knowledge and skills you will need to either prepare for specific occupational fields or to prepare more generally to enter many
career areas. For example, a major in engineering, education, or nursing will
require a concentration of coursework related to the practice of those professions.
A student who is inclined toward a more general education (liberal arts majors
such as psychology, geology, history) will take a wider variety of coursework
involving many subjects. Although business students will select a concentration of
courses within the business curriculum (e.g., finance, international business,
accounting), often the majority of coursework will be in many business subjects
so they are prepared to enter the broad range of opportunities that the business
world presents.

WHICH SHOULD I CHOOSE FIRST—A MAJOR OR AN OCCUPATION?

Actually, it doesn't matter! If you have a *strong* interest in a subject area such as psychology, marketing, or communication, choosing to concentrate in that major is a place to start. If you know you want to "be a respiratory therapist," then choosing that major is the path to take because specific knowledge and skills are required. *Most students, however, really don't know what is involved in their major until they experience the specific coursework that is involved.* In this way they either confirm their interest and abilities for the major *or* they might find that the experience isn't what they expected and decide to explore other possibilities. If you are undecided or have a strong interest in more than one academic area, it is probably best to spend some time taking a variety of courses in many academic areas before deciding on one. Community college students who intend to transfer to a four-year degree program after two years will need to plan carefully. Terminal two-year degree students will obviously choose a major upon entering college.

HOW IMPORTANT IS CHOOSING A MAJOR?

The importance that students place on selecting a particular academic major will depend on their career interests and goals. Some employers will tell you that your major is not that important unless very specific knowledge and skills are required for certain types of work. Many employers are looking for broadly educated college graduates who have the skills they are looking for, such as communication skills, demonstrated leadership qualities, relevant work experience (i.e., through internships, volunteer work, employment), and who can contribute immediately to their particular enterprise. If you wish to enter a two-year technical degree, however, then choosing a major upon entering college is very important.

HOW DO I BEGIN?

This workbook helps you move through a process of logical steps that lead to a major and perhaps a career decision. These steps are outlined in the model displayed in Figure I.1 on the next page. Although these steps are progressive, the process should be considered fluid. That is, the results of one step may indicate a need to return to a previous step if the desired outcome is not possible. For example, you might find that the course requirements in a major that appears interesting do not match your academic aptitudes and strengths. In this case, you might need to return to the "exploring majors" step to gather new or additional information. Or you may have made a commitment to a selective major but find you cannot enter it because you are unable to meet the criteria established by that academic department. In this case, you may need to return to the "taking stock" step in order to identify alternative academic majors that will match your proven abilities, accept much of the coursework you have already taken, and relate to general career areas you consider attractive. Another cause for reevaluation is if you discover as a four-year student that the area you wish to pursue is available only at a two-year college.

As you confirm or explore academic alternatives, keep an open mind for viewing information in an unbiased light. Also, be willing to work hard and be dedicated to seeing the task to completion. Although the decision about an academic major is not a simple one, the rewards for selecting a major that is realistic and satisfying will become apparent over a period of time. Through the activities, discussions, and assignments in this course, you will be setting important academic and career goals and creating a plan that will help you move toward graduation.

At the end of every unit in this book, you will be asked to discuss case studies of students who are making the same kinds of decisions you are making. Each case study illustrates a step of the process outlined in the model in Figure I.1. You will also be asked to keep a log to help you reflect and summarize what you have learned about yourself at each step of the way.

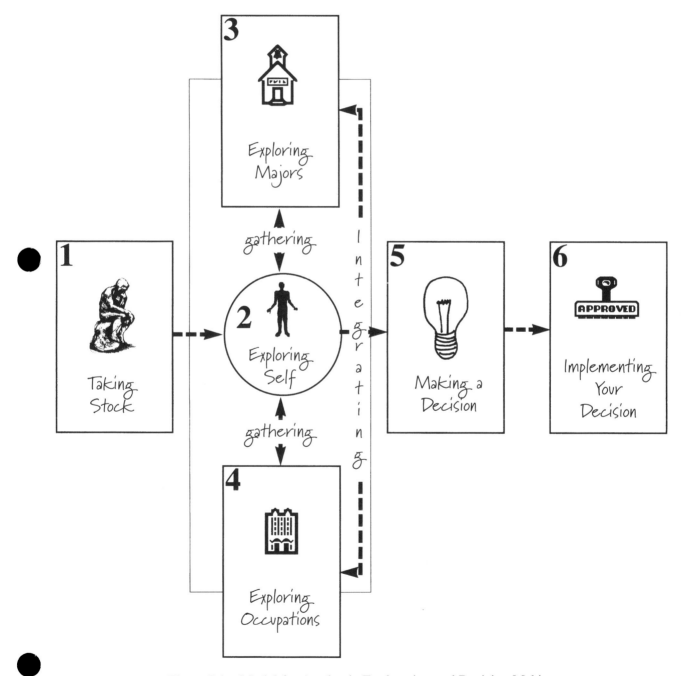

Figure I.1   Model for Academic Exploration and Decision Making

Selecting a College Major

UNIT ONE
Taking Stock

IN THIS UNIT, you will take stock of your current situation and examine how it has resulted in your decision either to be undecided about your major or to change it. This reflection will help you realistically evaluate past and present decisions and give you a foundation for exploring academic and career alternatives.

Taking stock is not always easy. It may involve looking at some frustrating or painful decisions you made in the past or at your inability to make a decision. Taking stock is vital, however, if you are to move on to the next step in exploring possible academic and career directions.

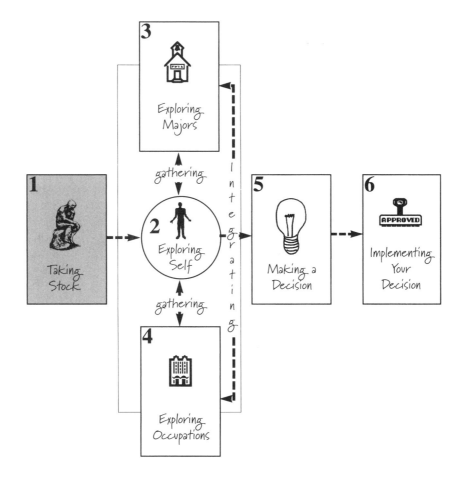

Two roads diverged in a wood, and I—
I took the one less traveled by,
And that has made all the difference.
From "The Road Not Taken" by Robert Frost

MAKING MAJOR AND CAREER DECISIONS

Whenever you are faced with two or more choices, you consciously or unconsciously use a process that usually leads to a decision. Because making decisions is such an integral part of daily life, learning to become an effective decision maker is important. Effective decision makers:

- Experience more personal freedom because they take advantage of new opportunities that appear
- Have greater control over their lives because they try to limit the influence of chance in determining their futures
- Are more likely than indecisive persons to be satisfied with their decisions

Educational and career decisions are among the most important decisions you will make, because these choices largely determine how you will spend your future waking hours. Some students entering college may have decided which occupation to enter after graduation but may not be sure which college major will best lead them to that goal. Other students may be undecided about a future occupational area and yet easily select an academic major. Still others are totally undecided about a major and an occupational choice; they have made a decision to be "undecided" about both.

Of those who declare a major upon entering college, some will later have doubts about their earlier decisions. There are many reasons for wanting to change majors: a lack of interest in the coursework, discouragement over poor academic performance, or inability to meet the criteria established for that major.

To help you begin the process of selecting a college major and/or career field, this unit asks you to take stock of your current status. This involves both determining where you are in the decision-making process and analyzing why you are where you are. In this way, taking stock lays the foundation for understanding how you personally will approach this critical endeavor.

As you complete the stock-taking activities in this unit, you will find some that are divided into two sections, "A" and "B." If you are undecided—that is, totally uncertain of your choice of major and/or occupation—answer the set of questions marked "A"; if you are considering a change of major or even having some doubts, answer the set of questions marked "B."

ACTIVITY 1.1: YOUR CURRENT MAJOR STATUS

Complete "A" if you are undecided; complete "B" if you are considering a change in major.

A. I am undecided about a major. (Check all that apply.)

❏ I don't have enough information about various majors.

❏ I don't have enough information about possible career fields to which majors may lead.

❏ I'm not sure about my ability to succeed in the coursework for certain majors.

❏ I have so many interests that I can't narrow my options.

❏ I don't have strong interests in anything, so I'm not sure where to begin exploring.

❏ I'm not sure of my values, so I don't know what is important to me in a major or career area.

❏ I'm afraid to choose a major because it might be the wrong decision.

❏ I'm not sure what jobs will be available to me if I graduate with a certain major.

❏ I have difficulty making decisions in general.

❏ Other people have suggested majors, but I'm not sure they are right for me.

❏ I realize now that instead of a four-year degree, I might want a two-year program.

❏ Other reasons (be specific): _____

_____

_____

_____

Examine the reasons you checked. In what areas do they indicate you need help (e.g., self, academic or occupational information, decision making)? Why?

_____

_____

_____

OR

B. I am considering a change in major or am having some doubts. (Check all that apply.)

❏ I didn't have enough information about this major when I chose it and have since found out it is not for me.

❏ I didn't want to enter college undecided about a major, so I signed up for one that seemed interesting at the time.

❏ I chose this major because other people strongly encouraged me in that direction.

❏ I discovered that the occupations related to this major do not appeal to me.

❏ I don't have strong enough abilities to succeed in the required coursework for this major.

❏ I'm not interested in the coursework required for this major.

❏ I'm not sure the values associated with this major (e.g., economic security) are as important to me now.

❏ I don't qualify for this program based on the major's entrance requirements.

❏ The major I want is offered at a four-year rather than a two-year college.

❏ Other reasons (be specific): _____

_____

_____

_____

Examine the reasons you checked. What influenced you to choose your last major? Are any of these strong reasons for you to explore other majors? Why?

_____

_____

_____

ACTIVITY 1.2: YOUR CURRENT CAREER STATUS

Complete "A" if you are undecided; complete "B" if you are considering a change in major.

A. I am undecided about an occupational field. (Check all that apply.)

❏ I don't have enough information about various occupations.

❏ I don't have enough information about the relationships between occupations and academic majors.

❏ I'm not sure of the abilities needed in certain occupations.

❏ I have so many interests that I can't narrow my options.

❏ I don't have strong interests in anything, so I'm not sure which areas to explore.

❏ I'm not sure of my values, so I don't know what is important to me in selecting an occupational field.

❏ I'm afraid to choose an occupation because it might be the wrong decision.

❏ I'm not sure what specific jobs will be available to me as a result of the occupations I am considering.

❏ I have difficulty making decisions in general.

❏ Other people have suggested certain occupations, but I'm not sure they are right for me.

❏ I'm not sure if the occupations for which I have an interest require a two-year or four-year degree.

❏ Other reasons (be specific): _____

_____

_____

Examine the reasons you checked. In what areas do they indicate you need help (e.g., self, academic or occupational information, decision making)? Why?

_____

_____

_____

OR

B. I am considering a change in occupation. (Check all that apply.)

❏ I didn't have enough information about this occupation when I chose it and have since found out it is not for me.

❏ I didn't want to enter college undecided about a major, so I selected an occupational area that seemed interesting at the time.

❏ I chose this occupation because other people strongly encouraged me in that direction.

❏ I discovered that the academic majors related to this occupation do not appeal to me.

❏ I don't have strong enough abilities to succeed in performing the work tasks in this occupation.

❏ I'm not interested in the work tasks involved in this occupation.

❏ I'm not sure the values associated with this occupation (e.g., working conditions) are as important to me now.

❏ I don't qualify for entrance into the major required for this occupation.

❏ I'm not sure if the new occupations I am considering require a two-year or four-year degree.

❏ Other reasons (be specific): _____

_____

_____

Examine the reasons you checked. What influenced you to choose your last occupation? Are any of these strong reasons for you to explore other occupational fields? Why?

_____

_____

_____

THE DECISION-MAKING PROCESS

Your Feelings About Decision Making

Whether you are undecided or considering a change in major, how you feel about making decisions in general plays an integral role in how you approach the process. Sometimes we ignore our feelings even though they may exert a strong influence on our decisions, consciously or unconsciously.

ACTIVITY 1.3: DISCOVERING YOUR FEELINGS

How do you feel now about choosing or changing your major? Place a check next to the adjectives that best describe your feelings:

❏ anxious	❏ disappointed	❏ frustrated	❏ pressured
❏ confused	❏ excited	❏ happy	❏ relaxed
❏ dejected	❏ fearful	❏ numb	❏ stressed

How do these feelings affect your motivation for engaging in the activities required to choose or change your major (e.g., When I feel stressed, it's difficult for me to feel motivated)?

_____

_____

_____

ACTIVITY 1.4: READINESS TO BEGIN THE PROCESS

As you begin this process of selecting a college major, it is important to acknowledge how ready or committed you are to the time and energy it will take. Sometimes we are motivated to accomplish a task because we genuinely want to have the satisfaction of accomplishing a goal. We can also be motivated because of pressure to make a decision from important persons or our institution. If you are not motivated or tend to procrastinate in the tasks necessary to choose a major, you will probably not complete the process.

(continued)

Place an "x" on the line below at the point that indicates your true commitment and readiness to engage in the process of choosing a major:

Extremely ready _____ Not ready at all

	1	2	3	4	5	6	7

If you have marked 5 or 6 on the line above, you will want to question your readiness to begin the process. If you marked 7, you should definitely reconsider becoming involved at this time.

Your Decision-Making Strategy

Theorists in the field of decision making identify different strategies people use when they are faced with both daily choices and more important but infrequent life decisions. The following activity lists strategies that several theorists have identified.

ACTIVITY 1.5: FINDING YOUR STRATEGY

Which of these decision-making strategies most closely resembles how you are approaching the decision of selecting or changing a major?

❏ **Procrastinator**—I know I must make a decision but will put it off as long as possible.

❏ **Impulsive**—I take the first choice that seems reasonable without looking at other majors or collecting information.

❏ **Fatalistic**—I will leave the decision to fate since I have very little control over it.

❏ **Agonizing**—I have invested so much time and thought into possible majors that I feel overwhelmed and can't decide.

❏ **Compliant**—I think it is best if someone else who knows more about the subject (e.g., parent, teacher, advisor) makes the decision for me.

❏ **Intuitive**—I will make a decision when it feels right.

❏ **Planful**—I will make a decision based on an orderly, rational process that requires solid information and reflection and involves both thinking and feeling.

How does the strategy you checked affect the way you did or will choose a major?

_____

_____

_____

If you checked a strategy other than "planful," what can you do to overcome any negative aspects of your approach?

_____

_____

_____

Your Decision-Making Style

Have you ever analyzed how you approach decisions? Over the years you have developed a personal decision-making style or set of behaviors that you use when confronted by a decision situation. Some styles are effective, while others may be counterproductive. You may use one style in major decision situations (e.g., choosing a major, buying a car) and a different style for smaller ones (e.g., what to wear, what to buy in the grocery store).

Decision theorist William Coscarelli determined that how you gather information and how you analyze it after you have collected it are important determinants of your decision-making style. You *gather* information either spontaneously or systematically; you *analyze* it either internally or externally. When these two dimensions are joined, four distinct decision-making styles emerge: spontaneous external, spontaneous internal, systematic external, and systematic internal.

- *Spontaneous*—You make a decision quickly, because it feels right; you know you can change it easily.
- *Systematic*—You collect all the necessary information first and then methodically weigh all the pros and cons before deciding.
- *External*—You talk with many people whose judgment you trust.
- *Internal*—You think about the situation and come to a decision on your own.

ACTIVITY 1.6: UNDERSTANDING YOUR STYLE

Now apply these dimensions to your decision making to discover why you are undecided or why you decided to change your major or occupation. *Complete "A" if you are undecided; complete "B" if you are considering a change in major.*

A. My decision to be undecided about a major and/or occupation was:

Spontaneous   **OR**   **Systematic**

- I changed my mind so many times, I couldn't decide.
- It just felt right not to make a decision.
- I know that once I decide, I may change my mind, so it's not that important.

- I collected a great deal of information from many sources, but still wasn't sure.
- I analyzed my skills and abilities to see how they matched certain majors, but I still wasn't sure.
- Once I make up my mind, I seldom change it, so I want to be sure before I make the decision.

External   **OR**   **Internal**

- I talked to my parents and friends about what to do.
- I consulted with my teachers and counselors.
- I considered the advice of others when choosing to remain undecided.

- I thought a lot about my situation before choosing to be undecided.
- I really didn't seek the advice of too many people.
- I examined all the information by myself but still couldn't decide.

(continued)

Circle the style you think you used in choosing to be undecided:

spontaneous external   spontaneous internal   systematic external   systematic internal

B. My decision to change my major and/or occupation was:

Spontaneous	**OR**	**Systematic**

Spontaneous

- My other major/occupation just didn't feel right.
- I lost interest quickly in my last choice and started to think about changing.
- If my next decision doesn't work out, I can always choose another.

OR

Systematic

- I examined my situation carefully and decided to change.
- I gathered a great deal of information about my situation before deciding to change.
- I know it will take careful study and thought before I can make a new decision.

External

- I talked to many people about my situation before deciding to change.
- I weighed the advice of others who knew my situation and decided to change.
- My friends encouraged me to change.

OR

Internal

- I am changing only after a great deal of thought.
- I thought about my situation for some time before consulting with others.
- I am still reflecting on my decision to change and will continue to do so.

Circle the style you think you used in deciding to change your major or occupation:

spontaneous external   spontaneous internal   systematic external   systematic internal

What do your answers suggest about how you tend to gather and analyze information before making a decision?

_____

_____

_____

Which style do you consider most effective in making realistic major and occupational decisions? Why?

_____

_____

_____

Occupational Stereotypes

Some like to believe that occupational stereotypes are a relic of the past. Today's reality suggests otherwise. For example, one in ten engineers is a woman, according to the U.S. Department of Labor. Occupational and academic stereotyping can exert significant influence on female decision making. From elementary school through high school, many girls learn from parents, teachers, and their peers that males are dominant or smarter in math and science while females are dominant in English and communication. Stereotyping begins early. In elementary school, when students are asked to draw scientists, both sexes draw males in white laboratory coats.

Males, to a lesser extent, avoid some occupations that society tells them are too feminine. For example, occupations such as elementary teaching and nursing are wide open for male participation, but males rarely are encouraged to enter these professions.

These subtle and not-so-subtle messages about appropriate occupations for each gender are found in textbooks, on television, in movies, and society in general. This sometimes results in girls avoiding math, science, and engineering occupations and males avoiding elementary teaching and nursing—even though both sexes have the ability and skills to succeed in all those areas. As you make decisions about your major and your future occupation, be certain to consider all options. Don't be afraid to take the road less traveled. Use the next activity to reflect on the stereotypical messages that may have influenced you.

ACTIVITY 1.7: REVEALING OCCUPATIONAL STEREOTYPES

Take a few minutes and list some of the messages you think you received about appropriate roles and occupations for females and males while growing up.

_____

_____

_____

_____

_____

_____

Do you think you have allowed these messages to limit your choices? Why or why not?

_____

_____

_____

_____

If your choices have been limited, plan to rethink your occupational options as you complete the activities in this text.

Your Goals and Decision Making

Setting short- and long-term goals is an important part of decision making. Without goals, you cannot estimate how your current choices will influence your future. In Unit Two you will examine your work values. Goals are simply values projected into the future, so identifying what is important to you will shape the major and career decisions you make now and in the future. Later, in Unit Six, you will be revisiting these goals.

ACTIVITY 1.8: SETTING YOUR GOALS

Think about the day after graduation and write down three goals you would like to accomplish by then.

Personal goal   (e.g., I will be a well-rounded, educated person.)

_____

_____

Academic goal   (e.g., I will graduate with at least a 3.0 grade point average.)

_____

_____

Career goal   (e.g., I will develop the skills and knowledge to be successful in the workplace.)

_____

_____

SUMMARY

As you read Unit One and worked through the activities, you took stock of your current situation and learned how your personal decision-making style has affected it and will affect it in the future. The stock-taking you did in this unit has prepared you for the next step in exploring possible academic and career directions. As indicated earlier, the decision-making process that you will be engaged in as you progress through this book is evolutionary, not static. You will gather information, identify alternatives, weigh them against your strengths and limitations, and ultimately decide on a direction to explore. You are in control of every aspect of this process.

SUMMARY

Check the appropriate column below to indicate how much you were aware of these elements in making previous decisions.

ELEMENTS OF DECISION MAKING	VERY MUCH AWARE	SOMEWHAT AWARE	NOT AWARE
1. understanding how I made past academic decisions			
2. understanding how I made past occupational decisions			
3. understanding my reasons for being undecided			
4. examining my feelings about making choices			
5. determining how ready I am to engage in the decision-making process			
6. understanding the decision strategies I use			
7. examining my decision-making style			
8. examining gender-role stereotyping in regard to myself and my occupational choices			
9. need for compromise when choosing between equally desirable alternatives			
10. importance of setting personal, academic, and career goals			

If you were somewhat aware of or not aware of some of these elements, be sure to emphasize these as you begin the process of academic and career planning.

CASE STUDY 1.1: ASHLEY
(for undecided students)

Ashley entered college with her major listed as undecided. She had so many ideas about a college major that she could not decide on one. She thought she could choose a major during her first year after taking a few courses. She was concerned that some of the majors she was considering, such as English and history, might not lead to a specific job. At one time in high school, Ashley had decided to be a teacher, because her mother was a teacher. Although she still felt this was a good profession for her—she would have the same hours as her children some day—she had never felt fully committed to the idea.

As a sophomore, Ashley finds herself no closer to a choice of major than the day she entered college and is feeling rather depressed and frustrated. She realizes she needs to take stock of her situation and take some action toward making a decision soon.

Certain ideas and people have influenced Ashley's occupational decisions in the past. What or who have influenced yours?

_____

_____

_____

Why is she undecided? Why are you?

_____

_____

_____

What are her feelings at this point? What are yours?

_____

_____

_____

Ashley's views of herself and/or occupations might be influenced by gender-role stereotypes. Could yours be too? How?

_____

_____

_____

To begin the process of deciding on a major, what could Ashley do next? What next steps do you need to take?

_____

_____

_____

CASE STUDY 1.2: MANUEL

(for students changing majors)

Manuel is a sophomore business major and is making average grades in his business courses. He chose business because he felt it would lead him to a well-paying job. Manuel finds, however, that he has no interest in his business courses and keeps putting off scheduling courses that he should be taking. He has become very involved in the theater activities on his campus by volunteering as a stage manager. He is also considering auditioning for a role in the next student production. Manuel is very excited about his involvement with the theater department and is seriously considering changing to a theater major. When he mentions this to his family, they are very discouraging. He knows he needs to take stock of his situation in order to decide whether to change majors.

What has influenced Manuel's ideas about occupational choices in the past? What has influenced *yours* the most?

_____

_____

_____

What are Manuel's feelings about his current major? About changing majors? What are *yours*?

_____

_____

_____

What compromises might Manuel need to make if he chooses a theater major over a business major? What compromises might *you* need to make?

_____

_____

_____

What can Manuel do to help himself decide? What can *you* do?

_____

_____

_____

PERSONAL LOG #1

A personal log gives you a chance to record and reflect upon thoughts, insights, and feelings about yourself and the steps you are taking toward making academic and occupational decisions. Following is an example of how one person's log might begin.

Sample Log

I never really thought about how I make decisions. I didn't realize how much I depend on the opinions of others when faced with a decision. I'm always afraid of making the wrong decision and think others know better than I do.

Also, I have never really tested myself. I don't know what I am capable of doing. I like math but I have never been motivated to spend the time and effort to do as well as I think I can. I feel that I accept second-best from myself. I am going to start demanding more of myself.

Write down any thoughts or feelings about your situation that taking stock in this unit may have prompted.

_____

_____

_____

_____

_____

_____

_____

_____

_____

_____

_____

_____

_____

_____

UNIT TWO
Exploring Self

> I should not talk so much about myself if
> there were anybody else I know so well.
> Henry David Thoreau

YOU ARE A UNIQUE PERSON, a unique blend of personality, interests, abilities, and values. Since self-exploration is a critical step in making realistic academic and career decisions, this unit will help you explore your personal characteristics. Deciding about a college major and a future career path are among life's important decisions—and the better you understand what is involved in this decision-making process, the better choices you will make.

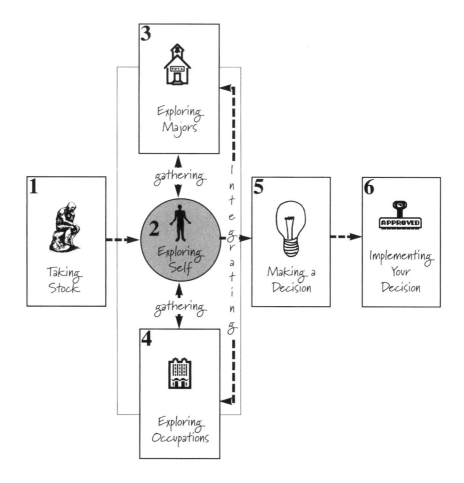

In this Unit you will:

- Learn how personality types might influence occupational choice
- Identify your occupational interests
- Learn about work values that are important to you
- Identify the skills you already have and those you may need to acquire

THE INFLUENCE OF PERSONALITY

Have you ever thought about how your personality might influence your educational and occupational choices? John Holland, a career theorist, has studied this idea in depth and suggests that your personality is reflected in the type of occupational environments or workplaces you choose. Holland theorizes that your personality is a product of both your heredity and your experiences, and that these in turn influence your preferences for a variety of activities and tasks. Your preferences develop into leisure and school interests (and later, work-related interests) that give you pleasure and satisfaction. As you engage in activities that are of great interest, you develop skills that later influence your educational and career choices. Note: If you wish to pursue Holland's ideas further, use the Web site www.self-directed-search.com or obtain a copy of *Making Vocational Choices: A Theory of Vocational Personalities and Work Environments* by John Holland (1997).

As a result of his research, Holland categorized workers into six personality types. He also divided all occupations into six work environments (using the same names as his personality types) in which these types of workers might be satisfied. He theorizes that people will seek work environments that are compatible with their personalities. Here are descriptions of Holland's six personality types:

- *Realistic:*   People with a realistic type of personality are conforming, frank, materialistic, persistent, modest, practical, shy, and somewhat hardheaded.
- *Investigative:*   Persons with this personality type are described as analytical, independent, intellectual, pessimistic, introverted, critical, precise, methodical, curious, and reserved.
- *Artistic:*   The artistic personality type is described as imaginative, creative, idealistic, expressive, intuitive, emotional, independent, and impractical.
- *Social:*   Social personality types are described as persuasive, insightful, extroverted, helpful, optimistic, and enthusiastic.
- *Enterprising:*   The enterprising type of personality is adventurous, energetic, pleasure seeking, extroverted, attention getting, ambitious, impulsive, sociable, and materialistic.
- *Conventional:*   The conventional personality type is persistent, conforming, conscientious, obedient, practical, orderly, thrifty, efficient, and somewhat inhibited.

ACTIVITY 2.1: YOUR PERSONALITY TYPE

Reread the Holland personality type descriptions above and write the names of the three types that are closest to how you would describe your personality:

_____   _____   _____

IDENTIFYING YOUR INTERESTS

An *interest* is a preference for certain types of activities. Generally, interests are learned. During your childhood and adolescence, you have acquired many preferences. You enjoy doing some activities more than others and prefer some tasks instead of others. The interests you have developed over the years will influence the academic and occupational paths you choose. Identifying your interests is an important step in beginning this process.

John Holland has developed interest inventories based on his theory of personality. The interest inventory below is reproduced from a version of Holland's interest inventory found at O*NET Resource Center (www.onetcenter.org), a Web site sponsored by the U.S. Department of Labor.

ACTIVITY 2.2: DEFINING YOUR INTERESTS

This activity describes various work activities that some people perform *in* their jobs. Read each description and place a √ (check) on the line next to those activities that you would *like* to do. Base your choices on whether you would *like* the activity, not whether you have the education, training, or skill to perform the activity.

Work Activities

_____   1. Build kitchen cabinets
_____   2. Design landscape areas for yards and parks
_____   3. Work on automobiles
_____   4. Solve mechanical problems
_____   5. Design computer hardware
_____   6. Study the physical sciences
_____   7. Work with animals
_____   8. Operate machines on a production line

Total √s in first 8 items: _____

_____   9. Study space travel
_____   10. Make a map of the bottom of the ocean
_____   11. Develop a new medicine
_____   12. Study ways to reduce pollution
_____   13. Diagnose and treat sick animals
_____   14. Study the personalities of world leaders
_____   15. Conduct biological research
_____   16. Study the governments of different countries

Total √s in items 9–16: _____

_____   17. Perform for a movie or television show
_____   18. Act in a play or movie
_____   19. Announce a radio show
_____   20. Write scripts for or edit movies, plays, or books
_____   21. Write reviews of books or plays
_____   22. Conduct or play in a symphony orchestra

(continued)

_____ 23. Create dance routines for a show
_____ 24. Draw or paint pictures

Total √s in items 17–24: _____

_____ 25. Perform nursing duties in a hospital
_____ 26. Help people with personal or emotional problems
_____ 27. Work with children or adults who have mental disabilities
_____ 28. Teach an elementary school class
_____ 29. Help people who have problems with drugs or alcohol
_____ 30. Organize activities at a recreational facility
_____ 31. Provide physical therapy to people recovering from an injury
_____ 32. Teach a high school class

Total √s in items 25–32: _____

_____ 33. Operate a company or business
_____ 34. Sell computer equipment in a store
_____ 35. Market a new line of clothing
_____ 36. Negotiate business contracts
_____ 37. Represent a client in a lawsuit
_____ 38. Start your own business
_____ 39. Develop an accounting system for a business
_____ 40. Design Web sites

Total √s in items 33–40: _____

_____ 41. Use a word processor to edit and format documents
_____ 42. Handle customers' bank transactions
_____ 43. Enter information into a database
_____ 44. Calculate the wages of employees
_____ 45. Assist senior-level accountants in performing bookkeeping tasks
_____ 46. Keep records of financial transactions for a business
_____ 47. Develop an office filing system
_____ 48. Transfer funds between banks using a computer

Total √s in items 41–48: _____

In the box below, record the number of activities you checked (√) "like" in each of the six numbered groups:

Item #s 1–8 _____ (Realistic)	Item #s 25–32 _____ (Social)
Item #s 9–16 _____ (Investigative)	Item #s 33–40 _____ (Enterprising)
Item #s 17–24 _____ (Artistic)	Item #s 41–48 _____ (Conventional)

Read the descriptions of the Holland occupational interest areas in Table 2.1. Circle the three groups in which you have the highest number of √s (checks).

Considering all these descriptions, write your three highest occupational interest areas on the lines below:

_____ _____ _____

Table 2.1 Holland's Six Occupational Interest Areas

Realistic: People with Realistic interests like work activities that include practical, hands-on problems and solutions. They enjoy dealing with plants, animals, and real-world materials, like wood, tools, and machinery. They enjoy outside work. Often people with Realistic interests do not like occupations that mainly involve doing paperwork or working closely with others.

Investigative: People with Investigative interests like work activities that have to do with ideas and thinking more than with physical activity. They like to search for facts and figure out problems mentally rather than to persuade or lead people.

Artistic: People with Artistic interests like work activities that deal with the artistic side of things, such as forms, designs, and patterns. They like self-expression in their work. They prefer settings where work can be done without following a clear set of rules.

Social: People with Social interests like work activities that assist others and promote learning and personal development. They prefer to communicate rather than to work with objects, machines, or data. They like to teach, to give advice, to help, or otherwise be of service to people.

Enterprising: People with Enterprising interests like work activities that have to do with starting up and carrying out projects, especially business ventures. They like persuading and leading people and making decisions. They like taking risks for profit. These people prefer action rather than thought.

Conventional: People with Conventional interests like work activities that follow set procedures and routines. They prefer working with data and detail more than with ideas. They prefer work in which there are precise standards rather than work in which you have to judge things by yourself. These people like working where the lines of authority are clear.

Record any other interests that you would like to add to the list above (e.g., from your leisure time, academic, or volunteer activities).

_____

_____

IDENTIFYING YOUR WORK VALUES

Values are those beliefs that are important to us and guide our choices and behavior. Your current values reflect the enculturation process that you have experienced thus far. As you have matured, you've modeled yourself after family members or other significant people in your life. Your family and significant others have reinforced the attitudes and behaviors that they hope will guide your life and influence your decisions. Honesty, independence, individualism, and personal responsibility are examples of values that may play important roles in your life and that you have learned from others. Values are central to the personal and career goals that we set for ourselves.

Work values are the values that you try to satisfy in your work role. The U.S. Department of Labor recognizes the importance of work values and describes six main work values in the discussion of occupations found at its Employment and Training Administration Web site (www.doleta.gov). A second list of work values is proposed by Farr, Ludden, and Sharkin (2001) in *The Guide for Occupational Exploration*. You have a greater chance of being satisfied with your eventual academic and career choices if you consider which work values are most important to you. To identify the aspects of work that are important to you, read the definitions of these major work values that are drawn from the sources cited above.

ACTIVITY 2.3: ASSESSING YOUR WORK VALUES

Circle the number that best represents the importance of each work value to you.

Achievement: You like to see the results of your efforts and feel you are accomplishing something.

Less important   1   2   3   4   5   6   More important

Autonomy: You plan your work with little supervision.

Less important   1   2   3   4   5   6   More important

Creativity: You like to create or design new things or present new ideas.

Less important   1   2   3   4   5   6   More important

Economic returns: You desire work that pays well.

Less important   1   2   3   4   5   6   More important

Independence: You do things on your own initiative and may even work alone.

Less important   1   2   3   4   5   6   More important

Intellectual stimulation: You like work that provides for ongoing learning.

Less important   1   2   3   4   5   6   More important

Recognition: You like to receive recognition for what you do.

Less important   1   2   3   4   5   6   More important

Relationships: You like to have colleagues who are friendly at work.

Less important   1   2   3   4   5   6   More important

Responsibility: You like to make decisions on your own.

Less important   1   2   3   4   5   6   More important

Service: You desire work where you can help other people.

Less important   1   2   3   4   5   6   More important

Social status: You enjoy being looked up to by others.

Less important   1   2   3   4   5   6   More important

Supervision: Your supervisors train you well and treat you fairly.

    Less important   1   2   3   4   5   6   More important

Security: You like work that provides job security and good working conditions.

    Less important   1   2   3   4   5   6   More important

Variety: You like to do different kinds of tasks at work.

    Less important   1   2   3   4   5   6   More important

List the three work values that you rated the highest:

_____   _____   _____

Are there other work values that are important to you? If so, add them on the line below:

_____

Work values can be loosely matched to Holland's occupational interest areas. In the right column of Table 2.2 below, circle the values you listed above.

Table 2.2   Occupational Interests and Work Values

Holland's Occupational Interest Area	Work Values
Realistic	Economic returns Autonomy Achievement
Investigative	Responsibility Variety Achievement Intellectual stimulation Independence
Artistic	Creativity Autonomy Intellectual stimulation
Social	Service Recognition Relationships Social status
Enterprising	Recognition Economic returns Relationships Variety Independence
Conventional	Security Supervision Economic returns

(continued)

How do your work values relate to your occupational interests?

_____

_____

_____

_____

IDENTIFYING YOUR SKILLS

Clearly, the skills you now possess and the ones you are willing to spend the effort to acquire will help determine the academic and career paths you choose. There is sometimes confusion about the difference between abilities and skills. *Abilities* are defined as our natural aptitudes or acquired proficiencies. *Skills* can be acquired and are capacities that facilitate learning or the more rapid acquisition of knowledge. Two- and four-year college degrees help you refine your basic skills and help you develop many others through coursework and out-of-class activities. At its CareerOneStop Web site (www.careeronestop.org), the U.S. Department of Labor has highlighted six sets of skills that are used in various work environments: (1) Basic Skills, (2) Complex Problem-Solving Skills, (3) Resource Management Skills, (4) Social Skills, (5) Systems Skills, and (6) Technical Skills.

The Department of Labor emphasizes that all occupational areas require Basic Skills. Knowing which skills are necessary to succeed in certain academic and occupational areas and the degree to which you possess them is an important consideration as you weigh your alternatives.

ACTIVITY 2.4: YOUR SKILL PROFILE

The skills identified by the U.S. Department of Labor, plus their definitions, are listed below. Each skill set has been divided into sub-skills to allow you to develop a comprehensive profile of your skills. Place a check (√) in front of the sub-skills in which you feel competent.

Basic Skills

_____ *Active Learning:*   Understanding the implications of new information for both current and future problem solving and decision making

_____ *Active Listening:*   Giving full attention to what other people are saying, taking time to understand the points being made, asking questions as appropriate, and not interrupting at inappropriate times

_____ *Critical Thinking:*   Using logic and reasoning to identify the strengths and weaknesses of alternative solutions, conclusions, or approaches to problems

_____ *Learning Strategies:*   Selecting and using training/instructional methods and procedures appropriate for the situation when learning or teaching new things

_____ *Mathematics:*   Using mathematics to solve problems

_____ *Monitoring:*   Monitoring/assessing performance of yourself, other individuals, or organizations to make improvements or take corrective action

_____ *Reading Comprehension:*   Understanding written sentences and paragraphs in work-related documents

_____ *Science:*   Using scientific rules and methods to solve problems
_____ *Speaking:*   Talking to others to convey information effectively
_____ *Writing:*   Communicating effectively in writing as appropriate for the needs of the audience

Complex Problem-Solving Skills

_____ *Developed Capacities:*   Having the capacity to solve novel, ill-defined problems in complex, real-world settings
_____ *Complex Problem Solving:*   Identifying complex problems and reviewing related information to develop and evaluate options and implement solutions

Resource Management Skills

_____ *Management of Financial Resources:*   Determining how money will be spent to get the work done, and accounting for these expenditures
_____ *Management of Material Resources:*   Obtaining and seeing to the appropriate use of equipment, facilities, and materials needed to do certain work
_____ *Management of Personnel Resources:*   Motivating, developing, and directing people as they work; identifying the best person for the job
_____ *Time Management:*   Managing one's own time and the time of others

Social Skills

_____ *Coordination:*   Adjusting actions in relation to others' actions
_____ *Instructing:*   Teaching others how to do something
_____ *Negotiation:*   Bringing others together and trying to reconcile differences
_____ *Persuasion:*   Persuading others to change their minds or behavior
_____ *Service Orientation:*   Actively looking for ways to help people
_____ *Social Perceptiveness:*   Being aware of others' reactions and understanding why they react as they do

Systems Skills

_____ *Judgment and Decision Making:*   Considering the relative costs and benefits of potential actions to choose the most appropriate one
_____ *Systems Analysis:*   Determining how a system should work and how changes in conditions, operations, and the environment will affect outcomes
_____ *Systems Evaluation:*   Identifying measures or indicators of system performance and the actions needed to improve or correct performance, relative to the goals of the system

Technical Skills

_____ *Equipment Maintenance:*   Performing routine maintenance on equipment and determining when and what kind of maintenance is needed
_____ *Equipment Selection:*   Determining the kind of tools and equipment needed to do a job
_____ *Installation:*   Installing equipment, machines, wiring, or programs to meet specifications
_____ *Operations Analysis:*   Analyzing needs and product requirements to create a design
_____ *Programming:*   Writing computer programs for various purposes
_____ *Quality Control Analysis:*   Conducting tests and inspections of products, services, or processes to evaluate quality or performance

(*continued*)

List four or five skills that you believe are your strongest:

_____

_____

_____

List skills that others (e.g., your family and friends) have identified as your strengths. Add these to your list, writing them on the lines below:

_____

_____

List the skills that you still want to acquire and what you can do to acquire them:

_____

_____

_____

_____

Some skills are associated with specific occupational interest areas more than others. Below are the six Holland occupational interest areas and the skills that are associated with each occupational area. Note that Basic Skills are required in all occupations.

In the right column of Table 2.3, circle the skills you identified above:

Table 2.3 Occupational Interest Areas and Associated Skills

Holland's Occupational Interest Areas	Associated Skills and Sub-Skills
Realistic	Basic Skills (e.g., Reading Comprehension, Science) Systems Skills (e.g., Systems Evaluation) Social Skills (e.g., Instructing) Technical Skills (e.g., Equipment Selection, Equipment Maintenance)
Investigative	Basic Skills (e.g., Critical Thinking) Technical Skills (e.g., Quality Control Analysis, Equipment Selection) Systems Skills (e.g., Judgment and Decision Making, Systems Analysis, Programming) Complex Problem-Solving Skills
Artistic	Basic Skills (e.g., Monitoring) Technical Skills (e.g., Equipment Selection, Equipment Maintenance) Social Skills (e.g., Coordination, Social Perceptiveness)

Table 2.3   *Continued*

Holland's Occupational Interest Areas	Associated Skills and Sub-Skills
Social	Basic Skills (e.g., Active Listening, Writing) Social Skills (e.g., Service Orientation, Instructing, Negotiating, Social Perceptiveness)
Enterprising	Basic Skills (e.g., Active Learning, Monitoring) Resource Management Skills (e.g., Management of Financial Resources, Management of Personnel Resources) Social Skills (e.g., Negotiation, Persuasion, Service Orientation)
Conventional	Basic Skills (e.g., Monitoring, Science) Systems Skills (e.g., Systems Analysis, Systems Evaluation, Judgment and Decision Making) Social Skills (e.g., Coordination)

Which occupational interest areas best reflect the skills you now possess or plan to acquire? How do these areas compare with the ones you identified in assessing your interests and values?

_____

_____

SUMMARY

In this unit you have identified and assessed important personal characteristics that will influence your academic and career choices. Knowing your interests, values, skills, and other personal preferences can lead to more informed academic and occupational decisions. Summarize how you would assess yourself at this point:

List three personality types that best describe you (Activity 2.1, pages 16 and 19):

_____   _____   _____

List your three highest occupational interests (Activity 2.2, page 17):

_____   _____   _____

List your most important work values (Activity 2.3, page 20):

_____   _____   _____

List your strongest skills (Activity 2.4, page 22):

_____   _____   _____

Write a short paragraph in which you summarize how your personality type, interests, work values, and skills might influence your major and occupational decisions.

Share your paragraph with someone who knows you well and ask him or her to give you feedback on your summary.

_____

_____

_____

_____

_____

_____

You will be using this personal information in Unit Three as you identify and explore possible academic majors, and in Unit Four as you explore occupational information.

Although this book is organized to explore majors first, if you prefer to explore occupational information first, start with Unit Four and then return to the major search in Unit Three. You can use either approach, but selecting a major first resolves an immediate decision that you are required to make. If there are specific occupations that you feel strongly about, however, gathering information about them first might be a better approach. You might be surprised at how many different majors can prepare you for certain occupations.

What limitations have you identified?

_____

_____

_____

How does this information about yourself fit with your past or current ideas about academic majors and career areas in which you may be interested?

_____

_____

_____

Internet Resources for Self-Assessment

Career Assessments.   You might want to use other career inventories to measure your interests, abilities, skills, personality characteristics, or work values. You can take the following inventories or surveys on the Internet:

- _The Strong Interest Inventory_   is administered from the publisher's Web site at www.cpp.com/products/strong.
- _The Self-Directed Search_   by John Holland is administered from the publisher's Web site at www.self-directed-search.com.

- *Campbell Interest and Skill Survey*   is administered from www.profiler.com/ciss.
- *The Keirsey Temperament Sorter,*   a personality-like inventory, can be taken at www.keirsey.com.
- *SkillScan*   is administered from www.skillscan.net.

Career Information.   The Internet has many of the most current sources of occupational information. The following Web sites specialize in databases and searches and include information about occupations, colleges, academic majors, scholarships, and financial aid:

- *O*NET*   (which has replaced the U.S. Department of Labor's *Dictionary of Occupational Titles*) is a database that describes more than 1,000 occupations in detail. It can be found at www.onetcenter.org.
- The *Occupational Outlook Handbook (OOH),*   published by the Bureau of Labor Statistics at the Department of Labor, provides extensive information on 250 occupations at www.bls.gov/oco. The *Occupational Outlook Quarterly* provides the latest information and projections on a variety of topics relating to the labor market at the same site.
- *America's Learning Exchange,*   sponsored by the Department of Labor, is a one-stop portal site to provide comprehensive career information, at www.alx.org. You can access America's Job Bank, America's Career InfoNet, and America's Service Locator from this site.

CASE STUDY 2.1: SABRINA

Sabrina is undecided about a major. She is very interested in sports but is not sure how to pursue that area in a major or career field. While she has participated in sports throughout her life, she knows she does not have the aptitude to be a professional athlete. Using the *Occupational Outlook Handbook* online at www.bls.gov/oco, Sabrina confirms her interest in sports. She is now considering a career in coaching, sports writing, or sports business. She knows she has the ability to do all three.

What other information does Sabrina need at this point? What do *you* need?

_____

_____

_____

Where can she obtain this information? Where can *you*?

_____

_____

_____

To move along in the choice process, what could Sabrina do next? What could *you* do?

_____

_____

_____

CASE STUDY 2.2: KEVIN

Kevin began his college work at a local community college where he majored in business management. Although he is doing very well academically, he isn't sure business is what he really wants. He is bored with economics and a business management course for which he is currently registered. His advisor suggests that he return to an important part of academic and career decision making: assessing his interests and strengths. When Kevin retakes some Web-based assessments, he finds that his highest interests and skills are in the arts/humanities area. He finds his strongest values to be creativity and esthetics. Kevin remembers all the art courses he took in high school and how much he enjoyed them. He is an avid photographer and has won local awards for his pictures. He wonders if he should change to a major that reflects his interest in art. He is concerned about the types of jobs he could get with such a major, however.

What other information does Kevin need to determine if an art-related major would be better for him than his current business direction? What information do *you* need?

_____

_____

_____

Where can Kevin obtain this information? Where can you find the information *you* need?

_____

_____

_____

To move along in the choice process, what could Kevin do next? What could *you* do?

_____

_____

_____

PERSONAL LOG #2

Summarize what you have learned from this unit and class discussions. What patterns are visible? What insights do you have about your interests, strengths, and limitations? What values have you identified? How are you going to use this personal knowledge?

_____

_____

_____

_____

_____

_____

_____

_____

_____

_____

_____

_____

_____

_____

_____

_____

_____

_____

_____

_____

_____

_____

_____

UNIT THREE
Exploring Majors

Seek for truth in the groves of Academe.

Horace

UNDERSTANDING THE MAJORS that are available to you is the next important phase of deciding on your future academic direction. Gathering information from primary sources is an important part of the decision-making process. In this unit, you will begin exploring majors from a broad perspective in various two-year, four-year, and graduate programs. You will also compare your interests with fields of study. You will then narrow down these possibilities to two or three majors that are available at your institution.

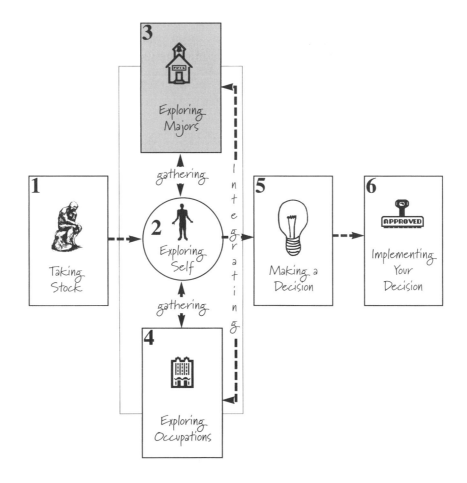

EXPLORING ACADEMIC MAJOR POSSIBILITIES

Understanding Degree Programs

Before considering possible majors, you need to understand how majors on your campus are organized (by college, school, or department) and how undergraduate degrees are created. The type of educational institution that you attend will determine the requirements for an undergraduate, technical, associate's, or baccalaureate degree.

An associate's degree may fulfill the general education course requirements for the first two years of a baccalaureate degree as indicated by the lower part of Figure 3.1, or may be a terminal degree itself. Some career and technical programs (e.g., culinary arts, massage therapy) do not require general education courses but focus strictly on the major requirements, as indicated by the top part of Figure 3.1. A two-year technical degree can provide the specific skills you would need to begin working in an occupation such as veterinary technology or construction management.

Most baccalaureate degrees require that students meet academic requirements in three general areas, as shown in Figure 3.2 and explained in the next few paragraphs. Generally speaking, basic or general education requirements are taken during the freshman and sophomore years, and departmental or college and major requirements are concentrated in the junior and senior years. In some cases a specific course may meet both a basic and a college requirement.

General Education Requirements.   The first area of requirements includes general or basic education requirements such as natural sciences, social sciences, and humanities. Such courses are intended to broaden your intellectual base and provide a stronger foundation for the specific subject matter in your discipline. General or basic education requirements are the foundation for the baccalaureate educational structure. Obtain a list of general requirements from your college bulletin or your instructor.

College or Departmental Requirements.   Requirements at the next level are generally viewed as departmental or college requirements. These usually involve

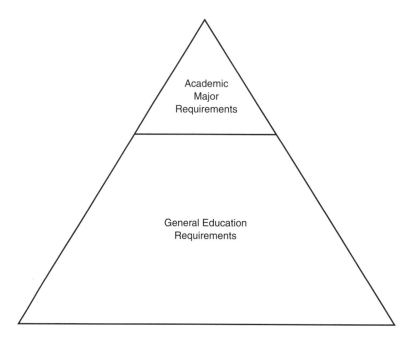

Figure 3.1   Example of an Associate Degree Structure

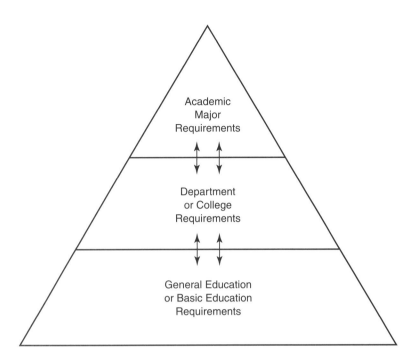

Figure 3.2   Example of a Baccalaureate Curricular Structure

more specific areas of knowledge, such as foreign language or mathematics. In Figure 3.2 this is shown as the middle layer. Obtain a list of departmental or college requirements from the department or your instructor.

Academic Major Requirements.   The final level of coursework is that required for the academic major itself. These courses provide in-depth knowledge pertaining to a specific discipline, such as history, architecture, business economics, philosophy, or even more specialized areas within such disciplines. In Figure 3.2 these courses fit into the top portion of the triangle. Obtain a list of academic major requirements from the department or your instructor.

Minors and Electives.   Some degree programs allow a certain number of credit hours to be used in coursework in another academic department that is designated as a "minor." These courses are viewed as broadening your knowledge in a completely different area or in a field related to your major. Other credit hours may be designated as "electives." These are hours counted toward graduation that are not part of majors or minors. (Some majors may "suggest" or prescribe that certain coursework be used to fulfill these elective hours.) Using these credit hours wisely can expand the breadth of your knowledge and help you learn about areas that are of personal interest.

Other Major Considerations

Degree Goals.   One important consideration when searching for major possibilities is identifying how your college degree will meet your personal, academic, and career goals. There is often confusion about the difference between a "liberal education" and a "liberal arts" degree. All college graduates receive a "liberal education" regardless of their academic major. This is based on the fact that most students, as indicated earlier, must fulfill certain basic requirements for a degree in addition to the coursework required for their academic major. Some students set a goal when they enter college to prepare for a specific career path that requires a more structured academic program (e.g., engineering, nursing, automotive technology). This is true for both a bachelor's and some associate's or technical degrees, as the subject matter is often related to the entry occupations associated with those degrees.

A "liberal arts" degree, on the other hand, involves a major in the humanities, sciences, math, the arts, or social sciences (e.g., history, chemistry, mathematics, art history, sociology). Some students prefer this broader approach to education because in most cases it allows more flexibility in selecting coursework and allows them to have more control over their academic experience. The requirements for some associate's degrees often include the same type of general or basic requirements that are in the first layer of Figure 3.2. Those students who continue in a four-year institution to obtain a bachelor's degree must also complete the courses that provide this foundation of academic coursework.

The Changing World of Majors.   Have you ever heard of a cheer worker, a weatherization director, a psychic counselor, or an interactive media planner? These are just a few of the new and emerging occupations that the U.S. Bureau of Labor Statistics (www.bls.gov) has identified. The academic offerings that past generations were able to choose have also changed and are still changing. Technology, for example, has created a need for more specialized majors or changes in the curriculum that reflect increasingly complex requirements for a new workplace. The names of majors change to reflect these new requirements as well. Evolution and Ecology, Health Information Management Systems, and Strategic Communication majors are examples. A Digital Design and Graphics major or a Chemical Dependency track in a Mental Health associate's degree did not exist ten years ago.

Personalized Study.   Another important opportunity in some institutions is for students to design a *personalized study program*. Although this option has existed for many years on some campuses, many students are not aware of its existence. Some students prefer to combine many different courses into a major they create rather than follow a prescribed track. A student interested in gerontology, for example, might combine coursework from sociology, psychology, business, health education, human ecology, and other academic disciplines. If you can't find a major that meets your specific intellectual needs and interests, check to see if this opportunity for a one-of-a-kind major is available at your institution and ask about the process for implementing it.

Study Abroad.   The globalization of work and other aspects of life today emphasize the need for students to develop the knowledge and skills that are required in an ever-expanding and changing workplace. Most colleges and universities offer study abroad opportunities and encourage students to take part in these programs regardless of major. Living in a different culture and speaking a different language can be a life-changing experience. Students should take the opportunity to study abroad when it is available—this experience can broaden both their educational and personal world perspectives and can be an advantage later when they begin their job search.

All of the considerations outlined above are important when beginning a search for a major that offers the best academic and personal fit. You will be able to incorporate these ideas into the activities in this unit, which are designed to guide you as you identify possible major alternatives and organize your search for academic information.

IDENTIFYING ACADEMIC MAJOR ALTERNATIVES

The framework to explore majors in this unit will be the *Classification of Instructional Programs (CIP)*, which is a taxonomic scheme of instructional programs used by the U.S. Department of Education. The CIP is used to track, assess, and report fields of study from the institutions of higher education across the country.

This section provides three different avenues for identifying the academic alternatives that you might want to explore:

1. *CIP areas of study:*   You will explore the complete list of majors identified by the CIP system. Even though the number of majors on your campus will be small when compared with the list identified by this government survey of all higher education institutions, check through the complete list anyway.

2. *Occupational interests matched to CIP areas of study:*   You will compare the occupational interests that you explored in Unit Two with the 14 Fields of Study that are part of the CIP system.

3. *Majors at your institution:*   You will examine the undergraduate majors available at your institution. From your institution's Web site, catalog, or from your instructor, obtain a list of the majors offered by your college or university. By checking the majors that interest you, you will identify several that you will want to explore further.

After engaging in these three approaches to identifying majors, you will be asked to synthesize your thoughts about the majors you chose. Pay particular attention to those majors that emerge on all three lists. These might be the ones for which you will want to gather more in-depth information.

CIP Areas of Study

As mentioned earlier, the Classification of Instructional Programs (CIP) is a tool that you can use to explore the various fields of study available in institutions of higher education. There might be some fields that you didn't even know about, or perhaps you didn't realize were taught in college.

The following activity asks you to explore the CIP areas of study to determine where your interests lie.

ACTIVITY 3.1: EXPLORING CIP AREAS OF STUDY

Check each area of study that holds or may hold some interest for you. If you do not know anything specific about the major, but the name conveys a positive feeling, go ahead and check it.

- ❏ Accounting
- ❏ Adult and Continuing Education
- ❏ Advertising
- ❏ Aerospace, Aeronautical Engineering
- ❏ Aerospace Science
- ❏ African American/Black Studies
- ❏ African Languages, Literature, and Linguistics
- ❏ African Studies
- ❏ Agricultural, Biological, and Biomedical Engineering
- ❏ Agricultural Business and Management

- ❏ Agricultural Communication/Journalism
- ❏ Agricultural Economics
- ❏ Agriculture, General
- ❏ Agronomy and Crop Science
- ❏ American Indian Cultural Studies
- ❏ Analytical Chemistry
- ❏ Anatomy
- ❏ Animal Behavior and Ethnology
- ❏ Animal Genetics
- ❏ Animal Physiology
- ❏ Animal Science

(*continued*)

❏ Anthropology
❏ Apparel and Textiles
❏ Applied Mathematics
❏ Arabic Languages and Literature
❏ Archeology
❏ Architectural Engineering
❏ Architecture and Related Services
❏ Architecture, Landscape
❏ Area, Ethnic, Cultural, and Gender Studies
❏ Art (Painting, Drawing, Sculpting)
❏ Art Education
❏ Art History, Criticism and Conservation
❏ Arts Management
❏ Asian Studies/Civilization
❏ Astronomy
❏ Astrophysics
❏ Atmospheric Sciences and Meteorology
❏ Audiology and Hearing Science
❏ Aviation/Airway Management Operations
❏ Bacteriology
❏ Biblical Languages
❏ Biochemistry
❏ Biology and Biological Sciences
❏ Biology, Cell
❏ Biology, Marine
❏ Biology, Molecular
❏ Biology Teacher Education
❏ Biomedical Communication
❏ Biostatistics
❏ Botany, Plant Biology
❏ Broadcast Journalism
❏ Business Administration and Management
❏ Business Statistics
❏ Canadian Studies
❏ Cell Biology
❏ Ceramic Engineering
❏ Ceramics
❏ Chemical Engineering
❏ Chemistry
❏ Child Development
❏ Chinese
❏ Chiropractic
❏ City, Urban Community, and Regional Planning
❏ Civil Engineering
❏ Classics
❏ Clinical Psychology
❏ College Student Counseling and Personnel Services

❏ Commercial Arts
❏ Communications Studies
❏ Community College Education
❏ Comparative Literature
❏ Computer and Information Sciences, General
❏ Computer Games and Programming Skills
❏ Computer Programming
❏ Conservation Biology
❏ Construction Engineering
❏ Consumer Economics and Home Management
❏ Corrections
❏ Counseling Psychology
❏ Creative Writing
❏ Criminology
❏ Crop Production
❏ Curriculum and Instruction
❏ Cytology
❏ Dairy Science (Husbandry)
❏ Dance
❏ Data Processing
❏ Demography and Population Studies
❏ Dental Hygiene
❏ Dental Laboratory Technologies
❏ Dental Specialties (beyond D.D.S. or D.M.D.)
❏ Dentistry
❏ Design, Applied
❏ Design and Visual Communication
❏ Developmental Psychology
❏ Dietetics
❏ Dramatic Arts
❏ Drawing
❏ East Asian Studies
❏ Ecology
❏ Economics
❏ Educational Administration
❏ Educational Assessment and Research
❏ Educational Psychology
❏ Educational Statistics and Research
❏ Education, Art
❏ Education, Early Childhood
❏ Education, General
❏ Education, Health
❏ Education, Higher
❏ Education, Kindergarten
❏ Education, Mathematics
❏ Education of the Deaf

❏ Education of the Emotionally Disturbed
❏ Education of the Gifted
❏ Education of the Mentally Impaired
❏ Education of the Multiply Impaired
❏ Education of the Physically Impaired
❏ Education of the Visually Impaired
❏ Education, Music
❏ Education, Physical
❏ Education, Reading
❏ Education, Religious
❏ Education, Remedial
❏ Education, Secondary
❏ Electronic Engineering
❏ Elementary Education, General
❏ Energy Management and Systems Technology
❏ Engineering, Aerospace, Aeronautical, and Astronomical
❏ Engineering, Agricultural
❏ Engineering, Architectural
❏ Engineering, Chemical
❏ Engineering, Civil, Construction, and Transportation
❏ Engineering, Electrical, Electronic, and Communications
❏ Engineering, General
❏ Engineering, Marine
❏ Engineering, Materials
❏ Engineering, Mechanical
❏ Engineering, Mechanics
❏ Engineering, Metallurgical
❏ Engineering, Mining and Mineral
❏ Engineering, Nuclear
❏ Engineering, Ocean
❏ Engineering, Petroleum (except Refining)
❏ Engineering, Physics
❏ Engineering, Technologies
❏ Engineering, Textile
❏ English, General
❏ English Literature
❏ Entomology
❏ Environmental Biology
❏ Environmental Design, General
❏ European Studies, General
❏ Exercise Physiology
❏ Family and Consumer Sciences
❏ Family Systems
❏ Farm Management

❏ Fashion Design
❏ Finance
❏ Fine Arts, General
❏ Fishing and Fisheries Science Management
❏ Foods and Nutrition (including Dietetics)
❏ Food Science and Technology
❏ Foreign Languages
❏ Foreign Language, Teaching English as a
❏ Forensic Science
❏ Forestry
❏ French
❏ Funeral Services and Mortuary Science
❏ Gay and Lesbian Studies
❏ Geochemistry
❏ Geography
❏ Geological and Earth Science
❏ Geological Engineering
❏ Geophysics and Seismology
❏ Genetics
❏ Government
❏ Graphic Design
❏ Health and Medical Administration
❏ Health and Physical Education
❏ Health, Public
❏ Hebrew
❏ Higher Education, General
❏ Histology
❏ History
❏ Horticulture Science (Fruit and Vegetable Production)
❏ Hospital and Health Care Administration
❏ Hotel and Restaurant Management
❏ Human Nutrition
❏ Industrial and Management Engineering
❏ Industrial Design
❏ Information Sciences and Systems
❏ Inorganic Chemistry
❏ Insurance
❏ Interior Design
❏ International Business
❏ International Relations
❏ Investments and Securities
❏ Islamic Studies
❏ Italian
❏ Japanese
❏ Jazz/Jazz Studies
❏ Jewish and Judaic Studies
❏ Journalism (Printed Media)

(continued)

- ❏ Kindergarten Education
- ❏ Korean Language and Literature
- ❏ Labor and Industrial Relations
- ❏ Landscape Architecture
- ❏ Latin
- ❏ Latin American Studies
- ❏ Law
- ❏ Library Science, General
- ❏ Linguistics
- ❏ Management, Business
- ❏ Management, Engineering
- ❏ Management, Fish, Game, and Wildlife
- ❏ Management, Hotel and Restaurant
- ❏ Management, Natural Resources
- ❏ Management, Parks and Recreation
- ❏ Management, Personnel
- ❏ Marine Biology
- ❏ Marine Engineering
- ❏ Marketing and Purchasing
- ❏ Materials Engineering
- ❏ Mathematics, Education
- ❏ Mathematics, General
- ❏ Mechanical Engineering
- ❏ Medical Laboratory Technologies
- ❏ Medieval and Renaissance Studies
- ❏ Medicine (M.D.)
- ❏ Metallurgical Engineering
- ❏ Meteorology
- ❏ Mexican American Culture Studies
- ❏ Microbiology
- ❏ Middle/Near Eastern Studies
- ❏ Mining and Mineral Engineering
- ❏ Molecular Biology
- ❏ Molecular Physics
- ❏ Mortuary Science
- ❏ Music (Liberal Arts)
- ❏ Music (Performing, Composition, Theory)
- ❏ Music Education
- ❏ Music History and Appreciation (Musicology)
- ❏ Music, Religious
- ❏ Natural Resources Management and Policy
- ❏ Neuroscience
- ❏ Nuclear Engineering
- ❏ Nuclear Physics
- ❏ Nursing
- ❏ Nutrition
- ❏ Occupational Therapy

- ❏ Ocean Engineering
- ❏ Oceanography
- ❏ Operations Management
- ❏ Operations Research
- ❏ Optometry
- ❏ Organic Chemistry
- ❏ Ornamental Horticulture (Floriculture, Nursery Science)
- ❏ Osteopathic Medicine (D.O.)
- ❏ Pacific Area Studies
- ❏ Painting
- ❏ Paleontology
- ❏ Parks, Recreation, and Leisure Studies Management
- ❏ Pathology, Human and Animal
- ❏ Pathology, Plant
- ❏ Pathology, Speech
- ❏ Peace Studies and Conflict Resolution
- ❏ Petroleum Engineering (except Refining)
- ❏ Pharmacy
- ❏ Philosophy
- ❏ Photography
- ❏ Physical Education
- ❏ Physical Sciences, General
- ❏ Physical Therapy
- ❏ Physics, Engineering
- ❏ Physics, General (except Biophysics)
- ❏ Physiology, Cell
- ❏ Physiology, Plant
- ❏ Plant Pathology
- ❏ Plant Physiology
- ❏ Play Writing and Screen Writing
- ❏ Podiatry (Pod.D. or D.P.)
- ❏ Political Science and Government
- ❏ Poultry Science
- ❏ Pre-Law Studies
- ❏ Psychology, General
- ❏ Public Administration
- ❏ Public Health
- ❏ Public Service, International (except Diplomatic)
- ❏ Public Utilities
- ❏ Purchasing
- ❏ Radio/Television
- ❏ Range Science and Management
- ❏ Reading Education
- ❏ Real Estate
- ❏ Regional Planning

❏ Religious Education
❏ Religious Music
❏ Religious Planning
❏ Religious Studies (except Theological Professions)
❏ Restaurant and Food Services Management
❏ Sanitary Engineering
❏ Scandinavian Languages
❏ School Psychology
❏ Science Education
❏ Sculpture
❏ Slavic Literature and Languages
❏ Slavic Studies
❏ Social Psychology
❏ Social Sciences, General
❏ Social Work
❏ Social Work and Helping Services
❏ Sociology
❏ Soils Science (Management and Conservation)
❏ South Asian Studies
❏ Southeast Asian Studies
❏ Spanish
❏ Special Education, General

❏ Speech and Rhetorical Studies
❏ Speech Pathology and Audiology
❏ Statistics, Business
❏ Statistics, Mathematical and Theoretical
❏ Student Counseling and Personnel Services
❏ Systems Engineering
❏ Teaching English as a Foreign Language
❏ Textile Engineering
❏ Textile Science
❏ Theological Studies
❏ Therapy, Physical
❏ Therapy, Recreational
❏ Tourism and Travel Studies
❏ Toxicology
❏ Transportation
❏ Transportation Engineering Management
❏ Urban Studies
❏ Veterinary Medicine (D.V.M.)
❏ Web Page, Digital/Multimedia, and Information Resources Design
❏ Wildlife Science and Management
❏ Women's Studies
❏ Writing
❏ Zoology

Now reread the items that you checked. Are there any patterns in common, such as interest areas, work values, or necessary abilities? Complete the following to help you identify patterns in your choices if they exist.

1. Record any of the majors that are science- or math-related (e.g., biology, mechanical engineering, statistics).

_____

_____

2. Record any of the majors that are oriented toward the social sciences (e.g., psychology, criminology).

_____

_____

3. Record any of the majors that are oriented toward the humanities (e.g., history, music, foreign languages, linguistics).

_____

_____

(*continued*)

4. Record any of the majors that incorporate business practices (e.g., computer science, economics, restaurant management).

_____

_____

5. Record any of the majors that lead to occupations primarily performed outdoors (e.g., forestry, horticulture).

_____

_____

6. Record any of the majors that lead to occupations that provide high salaries (e.g., medicine, finance).

_____

_____

7. Record any of the majors that require a technical degree (e.g., mechanical engineering, dental technology).

_____

_____

8. Record any of the majors that require a professional or graduate degree (e.g., law, dentistry).

_____

_____

9. Record any other patterns apparent from your choices (e.g., interest areas, work values, necessary abilities).

_____

_____

Which areas of study would you like to explore at this point? Identify at least five.

_____

_____

_____

_____

Why are you attracted to these majors?

_____

_____

_____

OCCUPATIONAL INTERESTS AND FIELDS OF STUDY

You have just explored all the majors that colleges and universities across the country have reported to the National Center for Education Statistics (NCES). The CIP has organized this large number of majors into *Fields of Study* that contain majors with common academic characteristics. The 14 Fields of Study that follow have been adapted from the CIP list to provide a framework for exploration. Read through these descriptions and circle those Fields of Study that sound the most interesting to you.

ACTIVITY 3.2: EXPLORING CIP FIELDS OF STUDY

1. *Agriculture:*   Instructional programs that focus on agriculture and related sciences and that prepare individuals to apply specific knowledge, methods, and techniques to the management and performance of agricultural operations
2. *Architecture:*   Instructional programs that prepare individuals for the professional practice in the various architecture-related fields and focus on the study of related aesthetic and socioeconomic aspects of the built environment
3. *Arts (Visual and Performing):*   Instructional programs that prepare individuals for professional practice in various art, music, and drama-related fields
4. *Business and Financial Operations:*   Instructional programs that focus on business and financial practices, research, and practical applications
5. *Communications:*   Instructional programs that focus on how messages in various media are produced, used, and interpreted within and across different contexts, channels, and cultures, and that prepare individuals to apply communication knowledge and skills professionally
6. *Computer Science and Mathematics:*   Instructional programs that focus on the computer and information sciences and mathematics and prepare individuals for various occupations in information technology, computer operations, and mathematical fields
7. *Education and Library Science:*   Instructional programs that focus on the theory and practice of learning and teaching, and related research, administrative, and support services
8. *Engineering:*   Instructional programs that prepare individuals to apply mathematical and scientific principles to the solution of practical problems
9. *General Studies and Humanities:*   General instructional programs or studies in the liberal arts subjects, the humanities disciplines, and the general curriculum
10. *Healthcare (Practitioners and Technical):*   Instructional programs that prepare individuals for all aspects of the healthcare professions, both as practitioners and technicians
11. *Legal Studies:*   Instructional programs that prepare individuals for the legal profession, for related support professions, and professional legal research, and focus on the study of legal issues in nonprofessional programs
12. *Natural Resources/Environmental Studies:*   Instructional programs that focus on the various natural resources and conservation fields and prepare individuals for related occupations
13. *Science (Physical and Biological):*   Instructional programs that focus on the biological or physical sciences
14. *Social Sciences and Social Services:*   Instructional programs that focus on the social and behavioral sciences, research, and the solutions to practical social problems

Keep the Fields of Study you circled above in mind as you engage in the following activities to help you identify majors within these areas.

ACTIVITY 3.3: MATCHING MAJORS TO FIELDS OF STUDY

Read the examples of academic majors categorized within the general Fields of Study that follow and place a check (√) beside each major that holds *some interest* for you (even if you know nothing about it). These are majors commonly offered by many colleges and universities. Note that a major may appear in more than one Field of Study.

Agriculture

_____ Animal Science
_____ Ag Economics
_____ Ag Communications
_____ Food Science and Technology
_____ Productions Operations
_____ Ag Business
_____ Horticulture
_____ Soil and Plant Science
_____ Ag Education

Architecture

_____ Architecture
_____ Landscape Architecture
_____ Architecture Technology

Art (Visual and Performing)

_____ Fine Arts
_____ Commercial Art
_____ Design
_____ Art History
_____ Art Therapy
_____ Arts Management
_____ Dance
_____ Theater
_____ Film, Video, and Photographic Arts
_____ Interior Design
_____ Art Education
_____ Industrial Design
_____ Music Performance
_____ Music Education
_____ Music History
_____ Music Composition
_____ Jazz Studies

Business and Financial Operations

_____ Accounting
_____ Computer and Information Science
_____ Finance
_____ Insurance and Risk Management
_____ Labor and Industrial Relations
_____ Real Estate and Urban Analysis

_____ Marketing
_____ Aviation Management
_____ International Business
_____ Transportation and Logistics
_____ Economics
_____ Business Education

Communications

_____ Journalism
_____ Public Affairs Journalism
_____ Broadcast Journalism
_____ Public Relations
_____ English
_____ Film and Video Studies
_____ Graphic Communications
_____ Technical Writing
_____ Communications Technology
_____ Advertising
_____ Communications Education

Computer Science and Mathematics

_____ Computer and Information Science
_____ Mathematics
_____ Statistics
_____ Actuarial Science
_____ Math Education

Education and Library Science

_____ Elementary Education
_____ Special Education
_____ College Teaching
_____ Secondary Education (see other areas for subject matter)
_____ Physical Education
_____ Sports and Leisure Studies
_____ Health Education
_____ Technology Education

Engineering

_____ Aeronautical and Astronautical
_____ Aviation

_____ Chemical
_____ Electrical
_____ Computer Science
_____ Civil/Environmental
_____ Agricultural
_____ Mechanical
_____ Industrial and Systems
_____ Materials Science
_____ Geomantics

General Studies and Humanities

_____ Ancient History and Classics
_____ English
_____ Foreign Language and Literature
_____ History
_____ Philosophy
_____ Area Studies (e.g., Women's Studies, Islamic Studies)
_____ Linguistics

Healthcare Practitioners and Technical

_____ Pre-Medicine
_____ Pre-Dentistry
_____ Pre-Optometry
_____ Pre-Veterinarian
_____ Pharmacy
_____ Nursing
_____ Physical Therapy
_____ Occupational Therapy
_____ Dental Hygiene
_____ Medical Technology
_____ Exercise Science
_____ Medical Dietetics
_____ Speech and Hearing Science
_____ Radiation Therapy
_____ Athletic Training

Legal Studies

_____ Pre-Law
_____ Paralegal Studies
_____ Criminology
_____ Law Enforcement

Natural Resources/Environmetal Studies

_____ Wildlife Science and Management
_____ Fisheries Science and Management

_____ Forestry
_____ Parks, Recreation, and Tourism Administration
_____ Environmental Science (e.g., Soil, Waste Management, Water)

Science (Physical and Biological)

_____ Chemistry
_____ Physics
_____ Geological Sciences
_____ Astronomy
_____ Biology
_____ Physical Geography
_____ Molecular Genetics
_____ Microbiology
_____ Zoology
_____ Entomology
_____ Evolution and Ecology
_____ Plant Cellular Biology
_____ Biochemistry
_____ Science Education

Social Science and Social Services

_____ Psychology
_____ Sociology
_____ Anthropology
_____ Economics
_____ Political Science
_____ Media and Communications
_____ Communications Technology
_____ Criminology
_____ Journalism (e.g., Public Affairs Journalism, Public Relations)
_____ Social Geography
_____ Social Science Education
_____ Social Work
_____ Public Administration
_____ City and Regional Planning
_____ Public Health Nursing
_____ Health Education
_____ Criminology
_____ Law Enforcement
_____ Fire Services
_____ Family Studies
_____ Human Development and Family Science
_____ Theology

(continued)

Record below at least five Fields of Study where you found the most interesting majors (e.g., Business and Financial Operations, Arts-Visual and Performing, Healthcare – Practitioners and Technical)

_____

_____

_____

The CIP Web site lists many more Fields of Study than those listed in this book. If you wish to explore majors by Field of Study directly on the CIP Web site, use the following directions:

1. Access the CIP Web site at www.nces.ed.gov/pubs2002/cip2000.
2. Click on "List CIP codes by 2-digit series" to obtain the list of Fields of Study.
3. From the drop-down menu, select a program area (Field of Study) in which you are interested. Click "GO."
4. Scroll down the list of majors in that Field of Study and record below at least five for which you would like more information.

_____

_____

_____

ACTIVITY 3.4: MATCHING OCCUPATIONAL INTEREST AREAS TO FIELDS OF STUDY

In Unit Two you identified preferences for a few occupational interest areas. In Table 3.1 you can examine how Fields of Study match these interest areas. (Note that some Fields of Study are compatible with several interest areas.) In Table 3.1, circle the Fields of Study in the right column in which you are interested.

Table 3.1   Occupational Interest Areas and Fields of Study

Occupational Interest Areas	Academic Fields of Study
Realistic	Agriculture Architecture Engineering Natural Resources/Environmental Studies Healthcare (Practitioners and Technical)
Investigative	Computer Science and Mathematics Engineering Science (Physical and Biological) Architecture General Studies and Humanities Healthcare (Practitioners and Technical)
Artistic	Arts (Visual and Performing) Communications General Studies and Humanities

Table 3.1   *Continued*

Occupational Interest Areas	Academic Fields of Study
Social	Education and Library Science Social Sciences and Social Services General Studies and Humanities Healthcare (Practitioners and Technical)
Enterprising	Business and Financial Operations Communications Natural Resources /Environmental Studies Legal Studies
Conventional	Healthcare (Practitioners and Technical) Business and Financial Operations Communications

Are the Holland types you preferred in Unit Two similar to or different from those indicated by your preferred Fields of Study? How?

_____

_____

Identifying Majors at Your Institution

In the previous activities, you have looked at all areas of study. Now you will narrow these down to only a few realistic undergraduate majors.

Obtain a complete list of undergraduate majors available at your institution from your college bulletin, through your institution's Web site, or from your instructor. In exploring college majors, you will not be able to examine details about every educational opportunity, so you must be selective in your approach. But first, from the list of majors available at your institution, identify at least five that interest you:

_____   _____   _____   _____   _____

Review your responses from the previous activities in this unit. Which patterns are evident from the majors you selected from your institution's list?

_____

_____

_____

_____

Now you are ready for the next activity, which is designed to help you narrow your search for a major.

ACTIVITY 3.5: SYNTHESIZING YOUR PERSPECTIVES ON ACADEMIC ALTERNATIVES

Thus far you have identified potential majors using three different methods. Record below the results of each of these approaches.

CIP Areas of Study (Activity 3.1)	Majors by Interest Area (Activities 3.2, 3.3, and 3.4)	Undergraduate Majors at Your Institution (page 45)
_____	_____	_____
_____	_____	_____
_____	_____	_____
_____	_____	_____
_____	_____	_____

Do any majors appear on all three lists? On two lists? Write them below.

_____

_____

Are two or more listed under any particular Field of Study? Which ones?

_____

_____

Finally, select three majors to explore in more detail:

_____   _____   _____

GATHERING ACADEMIC INFORMATION

Now that you have identified three appealing academic majors, you will want to explore them in more depth. The next set of activities will help you review your academic history to see how well prepared you are for the majors you have selected and how your past academic credits will work toward graduation requirements in these majors. (If you are a first term student you will be starting with a clean slate!) You will also gather information from other important sources that should shed some light on which majors seem the most feasible and attainable.

Activity 3.6: Analyzing Your Academic Transcript

Your past coursework can give you another perspective on the majors you are exploring. If you have had at least one term of school for which you have received grades, obtain a copy of your academic transcript. You will need to learn how to interpret it, as prospective employers may ask for information contained in it; each institution has its own method of writing a transcript.

Based on your transcript or your academic record thus far, answer the following questions:

1. How many credit hours do you have to date?

_____

_____

2. In which subjects did you earn your best grades? Why?

_____

_____

3. In which subjects did you earn your poorest grades? Why?

_____

_____

_____

4. Which subjects did you enjoy the most? Other than a good teacher, why did you enjoy them?

_____

_____

5. Can you determine some academic strengths from examining your transcripts?

_____

_____

6. Does your transcript reveal some academic weaknesses? If so, what are they?

_____

_____

7. How would you explain these weaknesses to another person (e.g., an employer)?

_____

_____

(*continued*)

8. Overall, do you see any patterns in your academic record that would indicate certain interests, strengths, or limitations for certain majors? What do you think is the reason underlying these patterns?

_____

_____

9. Are there any discrepancies between the majors you are considering and your grades in related subjects? Describe them.

_____

_____

It is important that the questions you have answered about your past academic work be considered realistically as you begin to narrow your options. (In Unit 6 you will use your transcript again to tentatively create a graduation plan.)

You are now ready to gather solid information about the major(s) you have identified from the previous activities.

Other Resources for Exploring Academic Alternatives

There are many sources for gathering further information about academic fields. Select one or more of the major alternatives you have identified and explore them in more depth through some or all of these avenues:

1. *Self-information.* A realistic assessment of your academic abilities will be helpful here. Consider your past experiences, including your academic preparation and your interest in certain academic fields.
2. *Firsthand experience.* Taking a course or two in the area you are considering will give you a very good idea whether this field is for you. You can also do volunteer or part-time work in an area relating to your major. If you are unable to volunteer or otherwise find work in the field, see if you can get permission to observe someone who actually works at a job you are interested in exploring.
3. *Printed materials.* Your institution has a wealth of printed information for you to consult to find out more about your academic field. Your college bulletin contains course descriptions that are especially helpful in describing upper-level courses. The major department has information about the major, including Web-based or printed materials. The career planning office will also have materials you can check.
4. *Computerized information systems.* Another excellent source of information is computer systems such as Discover and SIGI-PLUS that offer extensive, up-to-date information about the occupations to which a particular major can lead. Your instructor can inform you which systems are available on your campus.
5. *Internet.* As described in Unit Two, one of the most useful and accessible sources of information is the Internet. Many Web sites provide opportunities to assess your personal characteristics (i.e., interests, abilities, values) and to explore educational and occupational information. As noted previously, two excellent examples are the Department of Labor's O*NET Resource Center Web site (www.onetcenter.org), which gives information about many specific features of various occupations (including educational requirements), and the Web site for the *Occupational*

Outlook Handbook (www.bls.gov/oco), which provides detailed information about more than 250 occupations and their educational requirements. Your instructor can suggest other Web sites to explore for personal, educational, and occupational information. (Note: As with any source of information, care must be taken to evaluate the accuracy and timeliness of the information provided through the Internet.)

6. *Interviews.* Faculty members, advisors, college counselors, students enrolled in a major, and alumni who graduated with it—all are potential sources of information about this academic field. Interview guidelines and summary worksheets are provided for you on the pages that follow.

ACTIVITY 3.7: SEARCHING FOR INFORMATION ABOUT ACADEMIC MAJORS

Select one or more majors from your list and research them through your college's Web site, faculty, departmental offices, an academic advisor, or your institution's bulletin. Record the information you find in the summary sections that follow. As you gather information about them, keep an eye out for key terms related to the major that you can use in the next activity, "Using the Internet for Occupational Research."

Information Summary—Major 1:

Major: _____

Sources of information: _____

1. Department or unit where this major can be found:

   _____

2. What basic or general education courses are required for this major (e.g., English, math, social sciences, science, humanities)?

   _____

   _____

3. What basic courses in this major could you take to determine if your interests and abilities match?

   _____

4. Examine the upper-level courses listed in the catalog that are required for this major. List some that sound interesting to you. (Give course numbers and names.)

   _____

   _____

5. What is the *total* number of credit hours needed to graduate with this major? _____

   What is the number of required credit hours for the major itself? _____

6. What is required to enter this major (e.g., certain courses completed, application to a selective admissions area, certain grade point average, no requirements)?

   _____

   _____

(*continued*)

7. Other pertinent information about this major:

_____

_____

Information Summary—Major 2:

Major: _____

Sources of information: _____

1. Department or unit where this major can be found:

_____

2. What basic or general education courses are required for this major (e.g., English, math, social sciences, science, humanities)?

_____

_____

3. What basic courses in this major could you take to determine if your interests and abilities match?

_____

_____

4. Examine the upper-level courses listed in the catalog that are required for this major. List some that sound interesting to you. (Give course numbers and names.)

_____

_____

5. What is the _total_ number of credit hours needed to graduate with this major? _____

   What is the number of required credit hours for the major itself? _____

6. What is required to enter this major (e.g., certain courses completed, application to a selective admissions area, certain grade point average, no requirements)?

_____

_____

7. Other pertinent information about this major:

_____

_____

After you have gathered information about the major in which you are most interested, understanding some occupational relationships may help you decide to continue to explore this area. The next activity will guide you through that process.

ACTIVITY 3.8: USING THE INTERNET FOR OCCUPATIONAL RESEARCH

To explore possible occupational/career opportunities to which this major may lead, use the resources on the Internet to complete the following activity.

Make a list of key search terms that will be helpful in executing a search on a computerized information system or the World Wide Web. Some on your list might be *career, education, business*, or more specific terms such as the name of the occupation or major (e.g., *public relations, accounting*).

_____   _____   _____

_____   _____   _____

_____   _____   _____

_____

Once you have a list of key terms, find out which systems are available on your campus and how to use them—your instructor, a librarian, or a counselor at your career center should be able to help you get started. Summarize what you learn on the Internet Occupational Research Summaries that follow. Record what you learn about the occupations to which the majors you have selected can lead. Add your own questions to the summary sheet if they do not appear there already.

Internet Occupational Research Summary

Major 1: _____

Internet Resource or Computerized System Used (e.g., Internet site, Discover, SIGI-PLUS, other):

_____

Occupation 1 to which this major may lead: _____

1. Education/training required: _____

_____

2. Skills required: _____

_____

3. Some tasks involved in the work: _____

_____

4. Personal satisfactions: _____

_____

5. Employment outlook: _____

_____

6. Other information: _____

_____

(*continued*)

Occupation 2 to which this major may lead: _____

1. Education/training required: _____

_____

2. Skills required: _____

_____

3. Some tasks involved in the work: _____

_____

4. Personal satisfactions: _____

_____

5. Employment outlook: _____

_____

6. Other information: _____

_____

Internet Occupational Research Summary

Major 2: _____

Internet Resource or Computerized System Used (e.g., Internet site, Discover, SIGI-PLUS, other):

_____

Occupation 1 to which this major may lead: _____

1. Education/training required: _____

_____

2. Skills required: _____

_____

3. Some tasks involved in the work: _____

_____

4. Personal satisfactions: _____

_____

5. Employment outlook: _____

_____

6. Other information: _____

_____

Occupation 2 to which this major may lead: _____

1. Education/training required: _____

_____

2. Skills required: _____

_____

3. Some tasks involved in the work: _____

_____

4. Personal satisfactions: _____

_____

5. Employment outlook: _____

_____

6. Other information: _____

_____

_____

ACTIVITY 3.9: INTERVIEWING FACULTY, ACADEMIC ADVISORS, OR OTHER STUDENTS

One of your most valuable sources of information about the majors you are exploring is people who are knowledgeable about those areas. Locate at least two people who are familiar with the majors you are exploring—faculty members, academic advisors, or other students in the major—and arrange to interview them. Before the interview, write in the following spaces some of the questions you would like to ask. Take notes during your interviews in the space provided here. Then complete the Interview Summary sheets on the following pages to record what you learned. Add your own questions to the summary sheets if they do not appear there already.

Sample questions to get you started:

- Why do students select this major?
- What basic education courses would you recommend I take for this major?
- How much flexibility does this program have?
- What elective courses would be helpful?
- What are some other sources of information about this major?
- What kind of campus activities or student organizations on campus relate to this major?
- Does this major require or is it desirable to have a graduate degree in this area?
- What kind of careers are possible with this major after graduation?

Your questions about specific majors:

Major: _____

1. _____

2. _____

(continued)

3. _____

4. _____

Major: _____

1. _____

2. _____

3. _____

4. _____

Your interview notes:

_____

_____

_____

_____

_____

_____

_____

Interview Summary: Academic Major

Major: _____

Interviewee: _____

Title: _____

Department: _____

1. Prior to this interview, what were your assumptions about this major field of study?

_____

_____

2. What important aspects of this major did you discuss? Why are these important?

_____

_____

3. What did you learn about the course requirements for this major?

_____

_____

4. What are some positive aspects of this major? Negative aspects?

_____

_____

5. What did you learn about potential career opportunities in this area of study?

_____

_____

6. Based on the information you received in this interview, would you pursue this as a major? Why or why not?

_____

_____

7. What was your overall impression of the interview?

_____

_____

Interview Summary: Academic Major

Major: _____

Interviewee: _____

Title: _____

Department: _____

1. Prior to this interview, what were your assumptions about this major field of study?

_____

_____

2. What important aspects of this major did you discuss? Why are these important?

_____

_____

3. What did you learn about the course requirements for this major?

_____

_____

4. What are some positive aspects of this major? Negative aspects?

_____

_____

(*continued*)

5. What did you learn about potential career opportunities in this area of study?

_____

_____

6. Based on the information you received in this interview, would you pursue this as a major? Why or why not?

_____

_____

7. What was your overall impression of the interview?

_____

_____

SUMMARY

In this unit, you identified several academic alternatives that might interest you to some degree. You then explored these possible majors in more depth through several avenues of research. Now that you know more about the majors you chose to explore, what do you see as the pros and cons of each?

Major	Pros	Cons
_____	_____	_____
_____	_____	_____
_____	_____	_____
_____	_____	_____

List one or two majors that are the most promising at this point:

_____

_____

CASE STUDY 3.1: MARIA

Maria entered college undecided because she wasn't sure what was involved in different majors, such as coursework or jobs to which they might lead. She knew she was interested in the health professions, but she wasn't sure if she had the patience or the science background to succeed in any of them. She had volunteered in a hospital during high school and had enjoyed that work environment. Right now her strongest interests are in nursing, physical therapy, and pharmacy. She took chemistry and math her first semester and had a B average in both. Currently she is in her second semester of both subjects and has an A average. She has narrowed her ideas for a major to nursing and physical therapy and feels equally attracted to both.

What information does Maria need in order to narrow her options? What more information do *you* need?

_____

_____

_____

Where can she obtain this information? Where can *you* find this information?

_____

_____

_____

What specific action can you take now to move along in the process of deciding about a major?

_____

_____

_____

CASE STUDY 3.2: DUANE

When Duane entered college he was sure he wanted to be an engineer. He performed above average in math and science classes in high school, and his family always encouraged him to be an engineer. Duane is taking engineering-related courses during his freshman year, but is not enjoying them. Although he is studying constantly, he isn't doing very well in the core courses. He is not sure he would enjoy the type of work in which engineers are involved and realizes he knew very little about engineering when he chose it initially. Duane is becoming very discouraged and is considering a major change. He is getting his best grades in economics and English and enjoys both subjects very much. He hasn't discussed his situation with anyone, but he feels pressured to do something about it before he schedules courses for his sophomore year.

What kind of information does Duane need in order to decide about a change of major? What kind do *you* need?

_____

_____

_____

Where can he obtain this information? Where can *you*?

_____

_____

_____

What specific action can you take now to move along in the process?

_____

_____

_____

PERSONAL LOG #3

Record your thoughts and feelings about what you learned through exploring your different major alternatives in this unit. (For example, how does the self-information you gathered in Unit Two match the majors you identified in this unit? Do you have any possible future occupations in mind that will help you select a major?)

_____

_____

_____

_____

_____

_____

_____

_____

_____

_____

_____

_____

_____

_____

_____

_____

_____

_____

_____

_____

_____

_____

Mid-Course Instructor Interview

Make an appointment with your course instructor after you complete Unit Two or Three. List the concerns and questions you have at this point. Take this sheet and your transcript with you when you meet with your instructor.

1. _____

_____

2. _____

_____

3. _____

_____

4. _____

_____

5. _____

_____

6. _____

_____

UNIT FOUR

Exploring Occupations

> Your true pilot cares nothing about anything
> on earth but the river, and his pride in his
> occupation surpasses the pride of kings.
> > Mark Twain

AN IMPORTANT COMPONENT in exploring the majors you selected on page 56 in Unit Three is to consider their possible connections to future occupational fields and the needs of the future workplace. A recent study from the U.S. Department of Labor identifies three major trends that will shape the future of work in the 21st century: (1) shifting demographic patterns, (2) the pace of technological change, and (3) the impact of economic globalization.

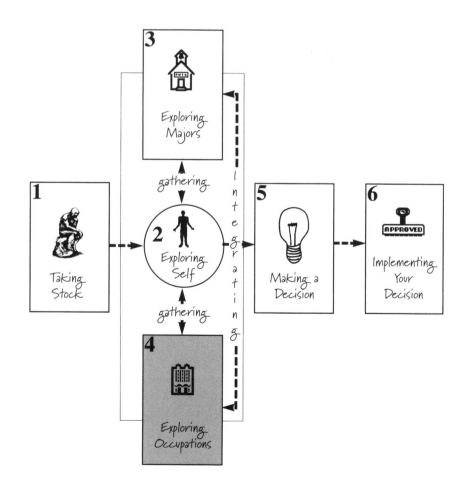

- *Demographics:* The U.S. workforce will continue to grow, but at a slower rate than in the past, and the workforce composition will be more balanced by age, sex, and race/ethnicity.
- *Technology:* The pace of technological change will accelerate in the next decade. Some of the advances will be in information technology (IT), biotechnology, and emerging fields such as nanotechnology. In the IT field, advances are expected in microprocessors that will support artificial intelligence, robotics, and real-time speech recognition and translation. Technological advances continue to increase demand for a highly skilled workforce.
- *Globalization:* The impact of economic globalization will be more extensive than before and will affect new segments of the workforce including some higher-skilled, white-collar jobs in the service sector, such as IT and business processing services.

These amazing changes in technology and the major impact of globalization present challenges to those who are preparing to enter the workplace. As a future worker you will need to be aware of this changing workplace, to know about today's technologies and most important, to be committed to learning the technologies of tomorrow. You should prepare to be self-reliant and a lifelong learner who accepts responsibility for developing your capacity to learn, to grow, and to innovate in order to be competitive in the global marketplace. In this context, it is important that you learn to be flexible and open to change.

Exploring occupations can impact your choice of major in two different ways. You can gather information about an occupation that requires specific knowledge and skills—such as physical therapy, electrical engineering, or elementary education. Alternatively, you can gather information about occupations that indirectly relate to majors such as biology, French, or philosophy—majors that provide more general preparation for entry into a variety of professions.

In this unit you will identify and gather specific information about occupations that interest you. You might also discover some occupations that are related to Fields of Study that you were not aware of in Unit Three. First you will identify occupations through two approaches; then you will perform information searches on these occupations.

IDENTIFYING OCCUPATIONAL ALTERNATIVES

When you were narrowing your search for academic majors in Unit Three, you briefly explored the ways that your interest areas, the CIP Fields of Study, and various occupations intersect. Now you will examine specific occupations more closely. The next two activities utilize two approaches to identifying prospective occupations.

ACTIVITY 4.1: REVIEWING OCCUPATIONS AND INTERESTS

Examine the following list of occupations that are organized by the interest areas you experienced in Unit Two. The occupations on this list are just *examples* of the many occupations in these interest areas. Some occupations appear in more than one area because worker interests and skills sometimes are relevant across fields or in a related field.

   Circle all the occupations that are interesting to you.

Realistic

Agricultural Engineer
Agricultural Inspector
Aircraft Mechanic
Animal Scientists
Architectural Drafter
Automotive Engineer
Chemical Engineer
Desktop Publishers
Electrical Engineer
Electronics Engineering Technician
Exercise Physiologist
Forest/Conservation Worker
Materials Engineer
Mechanical Engineer
Microbiologist
Oceanographer
Petroleum Engineer
Radiologic Technician

Investigative

Archeologist
Biochemist
Biologist
Chemical Engineer
Civil Engineer
Computer Programmer
Dental Lab Technician
Dentist
Ecologist
Economist
Electrical Engineer
Food Science Technician
Geologist
Horticulturist
Industrial Engineering Technician
Mathematician
Medical/Clinical Lab Technician

Meteorologist
Pharmacist
Physician Assistant
Physicist
Software Engineer
Soil/Plant Scientist
Statistician
Surgeon
Veterinarian
Web Site Developer

Artistic

Actor/Actress
Art/Drama/Music Teacher
Broadcast News Analyst
Choreographer
Composer
Dancer
Editor
English Teacher
Foreign Language Teacher
Interior Designer
Journalist/Reporter
Medical Illustrator
Music Director
Poet
Writer

Social

Air Traffic Controller
Counselor
Elementary Teacher
Fitness Trainer
Historian
Librarian
Licensed Practical/Vocational Nurse
Medical Assistant
Occupational Therapist

(*continued*)

Personal Financial Adviser
Physical Therapist
Private Detective/Investigator
School Counselor
Social/Human Service Assistant
Special Education Teacher
Speech Pathologist
Travel Agent

Enterprising

Advertising/Marketing/Public
   Relations Manager
Education Administrator
Financial Planner
Hotel Manager
Industrial Engineer
Industrial-Organizational Psychologist
Interpreter
Lawyer
Manufacturer's Representative

Occupational Health and Safety Specialist
Real Estate Agent
Real Estate Appraiser
Travel Agent
Urban Planner

Conventional

Air Traffic Controller
Auditor
Budget Analyst
Cartographer
Computer Operator
Computer Science Teacher, Postsecondary
Computer/Information Systems Manager
Financial Analyst
Insurance Underwriter
Kindergarten Teacher
Mathematician
Pharmacist
Tax Consultant

On the lines below, record the occupations that you circled above that are the most realistic and interesting. If you wish, add others that are not listed.

Occupation	Interest Area

1. How do these occupations fit with the interests, values, and skills you identified in Unit Two?

_____

_____

_____

2. How do these occupations relate to the majors you selected to explore in Unit Three?

_____

_____

_____

_____

ACTIVITY 4.2: REVIEWING OCCUPATIONS AND FIELDS OF STUDY

Record at least three Fields of Study that you identified in Unit Three:

_____   _____   _____

To find occupations that might relate to these Fields of Study, follow these steps:

1. Go to the Classification of Instructional Programs (CIP) Web site at www.nces.ed.gov/pubs2002/cip2000.
2. Click on "List CIP Codes by 2-digit series" to obtain the list of Fields of Study.
3. From the drop-down menu, select a program area (Field of Study) and click "GO."
4. Where available under the major, click on "Occupational Crosswalk" for a list of occupations for that major.

Repeat these steps for each Field of Study until you have identified some occupations to explore further and list these occupations below.

_____

_____

_____

_____

From the two lists, select the occupations that interest you the most at this point. Add other occupations that are not on the list but for which you would like information.

_____

_____

_____

_____

GATHERING OCCUPATIONAL INFORMATION

Now that you have identified some occupations to explore, the next step is to gather information about those occupations so that you can base your major and occupational decisions on solid, realistic, and current data. The activities that follow will help you know where to gather this information and help you frame the questions that will lead to a greater understanding of these occupations.

As you begin your search for occupational information, you may find the vast number of available resources difficult to narrow down. Because some occupational information may be more useful than others, the activities below are designed to help you get started. You might want to know what tasks are involved in the daily work, what qualifications you need to enter the occupation, who will hire you, and what is a realistic salary range. In addition, you might want other information, such as which occupations the U.S. Department of Labor considers the fastest growing (the "hotjobs"), which occupations will have the most future openings, or which occupations are declining in employment opportunity.

The activities that follow will guide you through the maze of informational resources that can provide answers to these and other questions. The Internet offers an amazing array of Web sites that provide occupational and related information in many formats. Although Activity 4.2 uses a specific Web information source, you will want to explore many other Internet sources as well. Here are a few that you might find useful:

- *O*NET OnLine*—a database developed by the Occupational Information Network under sponsorship of the Department of Labor: http://online.onetcenter.org
- *CareerOneStop*—a workforce information site sponsored by the Department of Labor: www.careeronestop.org
- *Career Voyages*—information about occupations, from a joint effort of the Department of Labor and the Department of Education: www.careervoyages.gov
- *MonsterTRAK*—a division of Monster.com, providing students and campus career centers with information about jobs and internships: http://campus.monster.com
- *Job Descriptions*—an Internet-based company that provides job information to the general public: www.job-descriptions.org
- *Yahoo! HotJobs*—a site with information for both employers and job seekers, including its popular consumer job board: http://hotjobs.yahoo.com

In addition to the Internet, there are other resources available for your occupational research:

1. *Self-information.* A realistic assessment of your academic abilities will be helpful here. Consider your past experiences, including your academic preparation and your interest in certain academic fields.
2. *Firsthand experience.* Internships or volunteer or part-time work in this occupation will give you a good perspective on whether you enjoy this type of work. If you are unable to volunteer or otherwise find work in the field, see if you can get permission to observe someone who actually works at a job you are interested in exploring.
3. *Printed materials.* Your library has a wealth of printed information for you to consult to find out more about your occupational field. Your campus career services office will also have materials you can check.
4. *Computerized information systems.* Another excellent source of information is computer systems such as DISCOVER and SIGI-PLUS that offer extensive, up-to-date information about the occupations in which you are interested. Your instructor can tell you which systems are available on your campus.
5. *Interviews.* Anyone who works in your field of interest is a potential source of information about the field. Interview guidelines and summary worksheets are provided for you in Activity 4.4 later in this unit.

ACTIVITY 4.3: EXPLORING OCCUPATIONS ON THE INTERNET

Select at least two of the occupations from your list on page 65 and research them in the U.S. Department of Labor's *Occupational Outlook Handbook* (OOH) using the following steps:

1. Access the Web site of the OOH (www.bls.gov/oco).
2. In the drop-down menu at the top of the page, click "Occupational Outlook Handbook," and then enter the name of the occupation for which you want information in the box at top-right. Click "Search."
3. Click on the different facts about the occupation and record your findings on the following pages.

Occupation Description

Occupation 1: _____

Sources of information: _____

  1. Nature of work:

  _____

  _____

  2. Working conditions:

  _____

  _____

  3. Education or training required for this work:

  _____

  _____

  4. Related academic majors:

  _____

  _____

  5. Employment outlook for this occupation:

  _____

  _____

  6. Salary range for this occupation:

  _____

  _____

(*continued*)

7. Related occupations:

_____

_____

Occupation Description

Occupation 2: _____

Sources of information: _____

1. Nature of work:

_____

_____

2. Working conditions:

_____

_____

3. Education or training required for this work:

_____

_____

4. Related academic majors:

_____

_____

5. Employment outlook for this occupation:

_____

_____

6. Salary range for this occupation:

_____

_____

7. Related occupations:

_____

_____

ACTIVITY 4.4: Interviewing WORKERS IN THE FIELD

One of your most valuable sources of information about the occupations you are exploring is people who are knowledgeable about those areas. Locate at least two people who work in or are familiar with the occupations you are exploring and arrange to interview them. Before each interview, write in the spaces below some of the questions you would like to ask. Take notes during your interviews in the space provided. Then complete the Interview Summaries on the following pages to record what you learned. Add your own questions to the Interview Summary if they do not appear there already.

Your questions about specific occupations:

Occupation: _____

1. _____
2. _____
3. _____
4. _____

Occupation: _____

1. _____
2. _____
3. _____
4. _____

Your interview notes:

_____

_____

_____

_____

_____

_____

_____

_____

_____

Interview Summary: Occupational Area

Occupational area: _____

Interviewee: _____

Title: _____

Place of employment: _____

(continued)

1. Prior to this interview, what were your assumptions about this occupation?

_____

_____

2. What important aspects of this occupation did you discuss? Why are these important?

_____

_____

3. What does this worker like about this occupation?

_____

_____

4. What does this worker dislike about this occupation?

_____

_____

5. Is this occupational area compatible with your work values (Activity 2.3, pages 20–21)?

_____

_____

6. What majors or training might lead you to this occupation?

_____

_____

7. What are three things you learned about this occupation?

_____

_____

8. Based on the information you received in this interview, would you pursue this as a occupation? Why or why not?

_____

_____

9. What was your overall impression of the interview?

_____

_____

Interview Summary: Occupational Area

Occupational area: _____

Interviewee: _____

Title: _____

Place of employment: _____

1. Prior to this interview, what were your assumptions about this occupation?

   _____

   _____

2. What important aspects of this occupation did you discuss? Why are these important?

   _____

   _____

3. What does this worker like about this occupation?

   _____

   _____

4. What does this worker dislike about this occupation?

   _____

   _____

5. Is this occupational area compatible with your work values (Activity 2.3, pages 20–21)?

   _____

   _____

6. What majors or training might lead you to this occupation?

   _____

   _____

7. What are three things you learned about this occupation?

   _____

   _____

8. Based on the information you received in this interview, would you pursue this as a occupation? Why or why not?

   _____

   _____

9. What was your overall impression of the interview?

   _____

   _____

SUMMARY

In this unit, you identified several occupational alternatives that might interest you to some degree. You then explored these possible jobs in more depth through several avenues of research. Now that you know more about the occupations you chose to explore, what do you see as the pros and cons of each?

Occupation	Pros	Cons
_____	_____	_____
_____	_____	_____
_____	_____	_____
_____	_____	_____

List two or three occupations that are still interesting to you at this point.

_____

_____

_____

Which academic majors might help you prepare for these occupations?

Occupation	Major
_____	_____
_____	_____
_____	_____

Case Study 4.1: Kim

After careful examination and thought, Kim has decided to transfer from her community college where she will receive an associate's degree in social and behavioral science to State University located roughly 25 miles from her home. Before making her decision, Kim looked at all the coursework involved in a four-year degree, interviewed faculty at State University, and talked with seniors majoring in psychology. She is also thinking about taking two or three business courses to expand her options after graduation. She talked with several people in the human resources (personnel) side of business with undergraduate degrees in psychology and found them to be satisfied with both their undergraduate major and their current careers. After exploring several Web sites to identify her interests and skills and reading about occupations, Kim feels she is making good choices.

What do you think Kim should do next?

_____

_____

_____

PERSONAL LOG #4

Record your thoughts and feelings about what you learned by exploring your occupational alternatives in this unit. (For example, how does the self-information you gathered in Unit Two match some of the occupations you identified in this unit? How do academic majors you identified in Unit Three relate to these occupations? Did you find possible related occupations that you had not considered before?)

_____

_____

_____

_____

_____

_____

_____

_____

_____

_____

_____

_____

_____

_____

_____

_____

_____

_____

_____

_____

_____

UNIT FIVE
Making a Decision

> Once a decision was made, I did not worry about it afterward.
>
> Harry Truman

YOU HAVE GATHERED a great deal of information about your personal characteristics, academic programs, and occupations. You now need to integrate this information in order to make a realistic and satisfying choice of major. If you are comfortable with the information you have gathered and the alternatives you have identified so far, you are ready to move on to step 5: committing yourself to one of your alternatives.

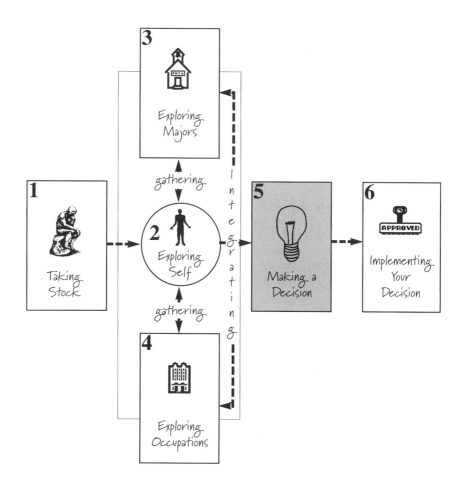

THE DECISION-MAKING PROCESS

Thus far in this book you have assessed your interests and abilities, learned about various academic options, examined your academic record, researched occupational fields relating to majors you are interested in, and perhaps reassessed an earlier decision. The most important part of your task remains: integrating all this information and analyzing it in order to identify a realistic academic choice. Each of the activities in this unit is one step toward completing this task.

ACTIVITY 5.1: LOOKING AT YOUR MAJOR CHOICES

List below all the majors you have identified thus far as being both interesting to you and academically attainable by you at your current institution.

Major	**Department, College, or School**
_____	_____
_____	_____
_____	_____

Do these majors have anything in common (e.g., all are social science oriented, all lead to one career area, all are within the same department or college)?

_____

Can you eliminate any of your major alternatives at this point? Why can you eliminate them?

_____

_____

_____

The Art of Compromise

An important factor affecting decision making is the art of compromise. If you are undecided, you may not be able to choose between two or more seemingly desirable major or occupational choices. You may not be able to decide because you want the "perfect" choice. If you are changing majors, you also might be looking for the perfect alternative. *Compromise* is a concession or an agreement to give up a desirable quality in one choice for a desirable quality in another choice. You may have to compromise between two majors, for example, that have equally desirable qualities. Or you may find that a compromise is needed because of some undesirable qualities within a choice.

As you move through the process of choosing a major, keep in mind that there are no black-or-white, right-or-wrong choices. You will be making a decision based on the best information available to you at that time. Developing the ability to compromise during this decision-making process might be required. This might mean examining the pros and cons of each alternative to evaluate the most desirable and undesirable qualities in each. Later in this unit you will be doing just that.

Consider this need to compromise as you progress through the decision-making activities in this unit.

Decision-Making Style

In Activity 1.6 on pages 7 and 8, you analyzed your decision-making style. Go back to that activity and determine if you have arrived at this tentative decision spontaneously or systematically. If you tend to be a spontaneous decision maker, it is hoped that this decision "feels right" and that you are ready to make a commitment, knowing that it can be altered or changed in the future. If this choice does not "feel right," you might want to retrace your steps to see what other majors you identified that are similar to this one.

If you are a more systematic decision maker, it is hoped that you are feeling comfortable with your choice knowing that you arrived at it in a methodical, organized way. If you are having second thoughts about this choice, you might want to retrace your steps to gather more information about other alternatives that you identified along the way.

Do you want to explore another major at this point? If so, which one?

_____

Return to the place in this workbook where you think you need more information (e.g., personal assessment, academic major exploration, occupational information) or need to reengage the process.

EVALUATING YOUR DECISION

To see how your work values fit with the occupations you are thinking about, and to assess which academic major would be best for that occupation, complete the next set of activities.

Matching Work Values to Occupational Alternatives

One important consideration in choosing a major is its relationship to your goals and future occupation. In Unit Two you identified some of your work values. Review these and decide which are the most important ones. Would you like to change any of these values? Also consider any values you identified from other sources (e.g., the Internet, Discover, SIGI-PLUS, interviews). When you are satisfied with your list, move on to the next activity.

ACTIVITY 5.2: NARROWING YOUR LIST TO REALISTIC ALTERNATIVES

In Unit Four, you identified some occupations that are interesting to you at this point. Now, record your most important work values in the first column along the left-hand side of the chart below. In the remaining blanks in the chart, record your occupational alternatives. Wherever one of your occupational alternatives fulfills one of your work values, place a check in the corresponding square. For instance, if one of your occupational alternatives is social work, and one of your values is altruism, place a check in the box where you entered "social work."

(continued)

Occupational Alternatives

Work Values			

Review the filled-in chart. Which occupation has the most checks?

_____

How does this occupation relate to the major you are considering?

_____

_____

_____

ACTIVITY 5.3: MAKING A TENTATIVE CHOICE

You are now at a point where one major should be clearly more desirable and attainable than the others. Check this major against the other information you now have.

Major: _____

Circle One		**Information**
yes	no	This major matches the interest patterns I identified in Unit Two.
yes	no	Occupations relating to this major are interesting and seem to be within my reach.
yes	no	My strongest skills are compatible with this major and related career areas.
yes	no	The work values I identified are incorporated into the occupations related to this major.
yes	no	The courses required for this major interest me.
yes	no	I have the ability to do the coursework for this major.
yes	no	The time it would take to complete this major is acceptable to me.
yes	no	If my major requires selective admission, I know the application procedures needed to be accepted.
yes	no	I currently have the grade point average (GPA) to be accepted in this major. (If no, is it realistic to expect to reach this GPA in a reasonable period of time? If not, what are the consequences?)
yes	no	I am more aware now of how I make decisions (how I gather and analyze information) and am comfortable with my "style."
yes	no	I feel good about my choice of major.

Did you answer yes to all these questions? If so, you are ready to test your choice against the force field analysis that follows. If not, what was your reason for answering no to one or more questions?

_____

_____

_____

_____

_____

_____

_____

_____

_____

_____

_____

_____

_____

_____

USING FORCE FIELD ANALYSIS TO ASSESS YOUR CHOICE

Kurt Lewin, a noted psychologist, adapted the concept of force field from the physical sciences to the social sciences. Although you have examined the pros and cons of past choices, the _force field analysis_ goes beyond that basic activity. When using the force field concept, you list the positive forces or reasons (pros) for your choice and negative forces or reasons (cons) against your choice. Now try to move the negative forces (those that are against your choice) from the right side of the line to the positive force field on the left side of the line. To change these negative reasons to positive ones, you must try to take some kind of action to alter them.

When there are more positive reasons for your choice than negative reasons, you have probably made a good one. If there are many more negative reasons than positive ones, you might want to rethink your decision.

The following case study demonstrates how a force field analysis worked for a real student.

CASE STUDY 5.1: KIM (REVISITED)

Recall from Unit Four that Kim decided she wanted to major in psychology. She checked her choice through a force field analysis:

FORCES FOR (+) A PSYCHOLOGY MAJOR ←	FORCES AGAINST (–) A PSYCHOLOGY MAJOR
Love the psych coursework Get good grades in courses Have wonderful faculty advisor Satisfies my interest in biology Able to assist with lab work Have time in curriculum to take some business courses Compatible with my values of helping people This major is intellectually stimulating	Too many psych majors—crowded courses Not enough time to take extra human resource courses May be difficult to find a job with this major Need a Ph.D. to be a psychologist

Kim found that she had more positive reasons to major in psychology than negative ones. When she examined the negative reasons, some were impossible to move to the positive side. For example, there is nothing she can do about the large number of psych majors, so she will need to accept large and crowded courses. She does not want to stay for an extra semester to take more human resource courses and she is not sure she will ever want to become a psychologist.

On the other hand, she has moved the negative reason about a job to the positive side by working with a career counselor in her campus career planning office. She discovered that psychology majors from her college have successfully entered a wide variety of jobs in many career fields. She is currently developing her job search skills to enhance her chances of obtaining a challenging job after graduation.

ACTIVITY 5.4: A FORCE FIELD ANALYSIS OF YOUR DECISION

Now test your choice of major in a force field analysis.

Name of major: _____

List the positive forces on the left; list the negative forces on the right:

FORCES (+) FOR MY NEW MAJOR ←	FORCES (–) AGAINST MY NEW MAJOR

Are there more forces *for* success in your new major than *against?* If so, you will want to make a commitment to your new major and continue through the remaining activities. If not, consider how you can change the negatives to positives. If you still have more negatives than positives, you may want to return to the previous activities and rework them.

COMMITTING TO YOUR NEW MAJOR

Congratulations! You have selected an academic major. Your decision was made on the sound basis of accurate and realistic information about yourself, academic requirements, and occupational options that attract you.

My academic major choice is: _____

It is in the department (or college or school) of: _____

My new major's departmental office is located at: _____

_____

           (Building)   (Street)

But you still have work to do. The remaining activities in this unit will help you with the details involved in committing to this major.

ACTIVITY 5.5: PLANNING YOUR ACADEMIC SCHEDULE

You now need to systematically plan future coursework for your degree and learn about the special services on campus that will help you with your job search later. You can obtain a checklist of requirements from the department or from your instructor.

Major: _____

Department: _____

Record below the courses you have already taken to complete the degree requirements for this major. List each course under the area that it fulfills and note the number of credit hours for each. (If you are a community college student, you may not have any department requirements.)

General Education Requirements			Department or College Requirements			Academic Major Requirements		
Course Title	Credit Hours	Grade	Course Title	Credit Hours	Grade	Course Title	Credit Hours	Grade
_____	_____	_____	_____	_____	_____	_____	_____	_____
_____	_____	_____	_____	_____	_____	_____	_____	_____
_____	_____	_____	_____	_____	_____	_____	_____	_____
_____	_____	_____	_____	_____	_____	_____	_____	_____
_____	_____	_____	_____	_____	_____	_____	_____	_____
_____	_____	_____	_____	_____	_____	_____	_____	_____
_____	_____	_____	_____	_____	_____	_____	_____	_____

(continued)

General Education Requirements			Department or College Requirements			Academic Major Requirements		
Course Title	Credit Hours	Grade	Course Title	Credit Hours	Grade	Course Title	Credit Hours	Grade
_____	_____	_____	_____	_____	_____	_____	_____	_____
_____	_____	_____	_____	_____	_____	_____	_____	_____
_____	_____	_____	_____	_____	_____	_____	_____	_____
_____	_____	_____	_____	_____	_____	_____	_____	_____
_____	_____	_____	_____	_____	_____	_____	_____	_____
_____	_____	_____	_____	_____	_____	_____	_____	_____
_____	_____	_____	_____	_____	_____	_____	_____	_____
_____	_____	_____	_____	_____	_____	_____	_____	_____

Total number of hours you have earned toward this degree so far: _____

Now list the courses you still need in order to complete this degree. Divide them into the semesters or quarters you plan to take them. If you think you have more than three semesters or quarters left in school, make photocopies of these pages.

Courses

	Department	Course Number	Credit Hours
1.	_____	_____	_____
2.	_____	_____	_____
3.	_____	_____	_____
4.	_____	_____	_____
5.	_____	_____	_____
6.	_____	_____	_____
7.	_____	_____	_____
8.	_____	_____	_____

Total hours this quarter/semester: _____   Semester/Quarter (e.g., fall, spring): _____

Cumulative quarter/semester hours: _____   Year: _____

Courses

Department	Course Number	Credit Hours
1. _____	_____	_____
2. _____	_____	_____
3. _____	_____	_____
4. _____	_____	_____
5. _____	_____	_____
6. _____	_____	_____
7. _____	_____	_____
8. _____	_____	_____

Total hours this quarter/semester: _____ Semester/Quarter: _____

Cumulative quarter/semester hours: _____ Year: _____

Courses

Department	Course Number	Credit Hours
1. _____	_____	_____
2. _____	_____	_____
3. _____	_____	_____
4. _____	_____	_____
5. _____	_____	_____
6. _____	_____	_____
7. _____	_____	_____
8. _____	_____	_____

Total hours this quarter/semester: _____ Semester/Quarter: _____

Cumulative quarter/semester hours: _____ Year: _____

How many hours are required to graduate with this major? _____

(continued)

How many hours do you still need to earn this degree? _____

What are the transfer or entry criteria to the department or college (if any)?

_____

_____

_____

What courses (if any) do you still need to take before you can transfer?

_____

_____

What other requirements, if any, do you still need to complete before you can transfer?

_____

_____

Are you interested in graduate or professional school? If yes, what are your reasons? What area(s) are you considering? What special criteria are there for entering this graduate program?

_____

_____

_____

_____

How do you feel about this major? Are you satisfied with it? Is it realistic and attainable? What courses are you looking forward to taking and why?

_____

_____

_____

_____

ACTIVITY 5.6: EXAMINING RELATED JOBS

The relationship between majors and occupations is obvious for some; for others, it is not. In order to explore the relationship between the major you have just selected and work environments to which it may lead, contact your campus career services office.

The career services office for this major is at: _____

_____

         (Building)   (Street)   (Phone Number)

Check the job postings at the career services office or other sources (e.g., Internet classifieds). Select two jobs that interest you and answer the following questions.

Job #1 Title and Description

_____

_____

_____

What qualifications are required for this position?

_____

_____

_____

How will you fit these qualifications after you graduate?

_____

_____

_____

Which of your work values can be fulfilled by this position?

_____

_____

_____

(continued)

Job #2 Title and Description

_____

_____

_____

What qualifications are required for this position?

_____

_____

_____

How will you fit these qualifications after you graduate?

_____

_____

_____

Which of your work values can be fulfilled by this position?

_____

_____

_____

Other Issues to Address

What experiences (e.g., work experience, extracurricular activities, volunteer work) will you need between now and graduation to enhance your chances of obtaining a position such as one of these?

_____

_____

_____

List three companies or institutions where employment opportunities for your specific interests may exist. For listings of such companies, consult your career services office, the Internet, the yellow pages, a career library, a computer job bank, and similar sources:

_____

_____

_____

ACTIVITY 5.7: ASSESSING YOUR JOB SEARCH SKILLS

Even though you may think graduation and searching for a job after graduation are far away, you will be developing critical workplace knowledge and skills during all of your college years.

Rate your job search skills on the chart below. You need to work on upgrading any skill that you do not rate "excellent." Depending on which skill it is, you might contact your career services office, attend a resume-writing workshop, practice interviewing with a classmate, or explore internship opportunities. The Appendix contains sample resumes and a resume-writing exercise for you to complete if you need to, as well as information on cover letters and interviewing skills.

Skill	Excellent	Good	Poor
Knowledge of co-op or internship opportunities			
Writing resumes			
Writing cover letters			
Interviewing techniques			
Knowledge of job search resources on your campus			
Knowledge of job search resources in your community			

Write down the skills you rated "good" or "poor," and indicate what you can do now to improve these skills:

Skill	Improvement Action

SUMMARY

In this unit you examined your alternative majors carefully in terms of your work values and other personal information. You have now made a commitment to a major and formed a graduation plan. You have also learned how this major relates to possible career directions.

Now that you have made a decision, you will need to complete the process by implementing that decision. Unit Six will help you establish a plan of action to accomplish this.

CASE STUDY 5.2: ROBERT

After a concentrated exploration process, Robert has decided on an education major in social studies. He has thought about being a teacher for some time, and all the personal, academic, and occupational information he has collected confirms this decision. He has also thought about entering law school someday, because he thinks the field of educational law is a fascinating and important one. Robert has carefully organized a graduation plan to be his guide for the next two years. He is doing extremely well academically, so he has no doubt about his ability to complete his goal. He has looked at the job possibilities in education and is confident he will be able to find a position as a high school social studies teacher after graduation. He has put together a tentative resume and intends to enlarge his scope of experience with children during the next two years.

What are Robert's next steps in order to implement this plan? What next steps do *you* need to take?

_____

_____

_____

_____

_____

_____

_____

_____

_____

_____

_____

_____

_____

_____

_____

_____

PERSONAL LOG #5

Summarize what you have learned from this unit and class discussions. How do you feel about making a commitment to a major? Have you ever made a commitment to an educational or career choice before? How is this decision different from past ones? How will you make future commitments?

_____

_____

_____

_____

_____

_____

_____

_____

_____

_____

_____

_____

_____

_____

_____

_____

_____

_____

_____

UNIT SIX

Implementing Your Decision

What the future has in store for you depends
largely on what you place in store for the future.

Anonymous

YOU ARE NOW READY to implement the decision you made in Unit Five and begin working with your new major. No decision is complete, however, until the first step toward fulfilling it is taken. There are initial actions you need to take and goals you need to set for future actions. Perhaps most important, you need to realize that no decision is set in stone; decisions you make today can always be changed tomorrow.

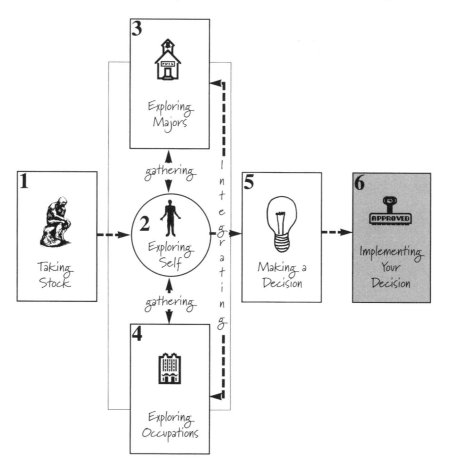

ACTION PLANNING

Now that you have chosen a major, you need to put your decision into action. The activities in this unit will assist you in implementing your decision in a satisfying and efficient way.

I have made a commitment to pursue the following major: _____

ACTIVITY 6.1: TAKING IMMEDIATE ACTION

There are several possible actions you can take to complete your decision. Check the action you intend to take now:

❏ Transfer to the department or college in my institution where my new major is located.
❏ Stay where I am until I can complete the requirements necessary to enter my new major.
❏ Enroll in another institution (e.g., university, community college, technical school).

❏ Stop my enrollment in college for awhile.
❏ Other (please specify): _____
_____
_____

Whichever action you checked, you will need to take specific steps to accomplish it. Break down the action into its component steps and write them here. (e.g., To enroll in my new major I will call my academic advisor to find out what procedures are required.)

1. _____

2. _____

3. _____

4. _____

5. _____

GOAL SETTING

As you take action to implement your decision, it is time to think about the future and the actions you will want to take now to prepare for when you leave college after graduation. This involves setting short- and long-term academic, career, and personal goals. In Activity 1.8 in Unit One (page 10), you wrote three goals you would like to accomplish by graduation. Review them before completing the following goal-setting activities to determine if they are still viable or if you wish to change them.

ACTIVITY 6.2: SETTING ACADEMIC GOALS

Now that you have outlined the action steps you need to take to implement your decision about a major, there are certain academic goals that you will want to set. Write your goals in specific, action-oriented terms. What do you need to do to make these goals come true?

Write a short-term *academic* **goal** (e.g., Within the next two weeks I will sit down with my academic advisor and plan the coursework in my new major for each semester until graduation):

_____

_____

_____

Steps I will take to implement this goal (e.g., I will phone my advisor for an appointment today):

_____

_____

_____

Write a long-term *academic* **goal** (e.g., I will graduate with at least an A-minus average in all my major courses):

_____

_____

_____

Steps I will take to implement this goal (e.g., I will improve my study habits and spend more time preparing for each class):

_____

_____

_____

ACTIVITY 6.3: SETTING CAREER GOALS

Although your academic goals are the most obvious part of fulfilling your commitment to your new major, thinking about your short- and long-term career goals is just as important as you progress toward your college degree. You might want to consider the work values that you chose in Activity 2.3 on pages 20–22 as you set your career and personal goals.

Write a short-term *career* **goal** (e.g., I will put together a resume based on my experiences up to now):

_____

_____

Steps I will take to implement this goal (e.g., I will visit the campus career planning office tomorrow to use their resume-writing resources):

_____

_____

Write a long-term *career* **goal** (e.g., I will find a job after graduation that offers me personal satisfaction and has good prospects for my future):

_____

_____

Steps I will take to implement this goal (e.g., I will look into internship opportunities relating to my major and find out what is involved in taking part):

_____

_____

ACTIVITY 6.4: SETTING PERSONAL GOALS

Setting academic and career goals involves your personal needs and goals as well. Being successful in your academic and career life gives you personal confidence and satisfaction. Setting personal goals requires self-examination and reflection. What kind of person do you want to be when you graduate?

Write a short-term *personal* **goal** (e.g., I will improve how I manage my time):

_____

_____

Steps I will take to implement this goal (e.g., I will sign up for a time management workshop that is offered at our campus counseling center):

_____

_____

Write a long-term _personal_ **goal** (e.g., By the time I graduate I will have taken advantage of the cultural and social opportunities offered on campus so that I can become a truly "educated person"):

_____

_____

Steps I will take to implement this goal (e.g., I will check the college Web site every week to see what lectures, concerts, theater productions, etc., I might want to attend):

_____

_____

Other academic, career, and personal goals I want to set:

_____

_____

ACTIVITY 6.5: REEXAMINING PREVIOUS GOALS

In Activity 1.8 in Unit One, you wrote down some general goals you would like to accomplish by the day after graduation (see page 10).

Reexamine these goals to see if you would like to keep, change, or embellish them. Write your thoughts here.

_____

_____

How are your present goals _similar_ to the previous goals you set?

_____

_____

How are your present goals _different_ from the previous goals you set?

_____

_____

(_continued_)

Has the work you have completed in this course changed the way you view your academic goals? Career goals? Personal goals? If so, how?

_____

_____

_____

PERIODIC REASSESSMENT

Although you have chosen a major and set goals that seem satisfying and attainable, new information or events in your life may necessitate periodic reassessment of your decision. This is the nature of decision making. For instance, the coursework in your new major may not be as interesting as you thought it would be; your graduation plan may need adjustments after you take a few courses or begin your job search. Every decision is open to change and adjustment as you live with it.

There are no right or wrong decisions—just decisions that may or may not need to be altered down the road. Whether a decision is good or bad is based on how the decision is made, not on how the decision turns out. A good decision can, and often does, lead to a poor outcome, because external events that affect the decision are frequently beyond your control. This is why periodic reassessment of all your decisions is important.

SUMMARY

Congratulations! You have just completed the very important process of choosing a major. You have assessed your personal needs, gathered and analyzed information, and made a decision. You have now begun to take steps to implement your decision and set goals for the near and far future.

If you need to make adjustments later, you will be ready to make them. Remember that when you take control of the decision-making process, your chances of making choices that are personally satisfying and attainable are greatly enhanced.

CASE STUDY 6.1: YOU

Write a case study about yourself and how you explored various academic options and finally made a decision during this course (approximately 400 words or two double-spaced, typed pages). Describe how you felt at the beginning when you took stock of your situation. How did you feel as you gathered information about yourself, majors, and occupations? What aspects of that stage did you like the best? The least? How did you feel when you made a commitment to a major? What happened when you took the steps to implement that decision? How will you make educational and career decisions in the future?

_____

_____

_____

_____

_____

_____

_____

_____

_____

_____

_____

_____

_____

_____

_____

_____

_____

_____

APPENDIX

The Job Search: Resumes, Cover Letters, and Interview Preparation

ALTHOUGH YOU MAY THINK it is too soon to think about developing job search skills, career experts will tell you that preparing for a job after graduation should begin your first year in college.

In Unit Five, you visited a career services office to identify and explore jobs that interested you and that were related to your major. This is an important first step in preparing for a job search, but there are others, such as preparing a resume to inform potential employers of your qualifications, writing cover letters to accompany your resume or job application or to inquire about employment, developing your interviewing skills, and requesting letters of recommendation.

This appendix is intended only as a brief introduction to some of the job search skills you will need to acquire during your college years. You will have the opportunity to write a first-draft resume, learn what should be included in a cover letter, and review your skills as an interviewee. Your campus career services office probably has workshops or classes to help develop your proficiency in these and other aspects of the job search process. Remember, your campus career services office is a valuable resource in preparing for the workforce. Don't wait until your senior year to make contact!

RESUMES

In completing the exercises in this workbook, you have had a chance to compile considerable information about yourself. Now is the time to organize this in the form of a resume for future use. A *resume* is a document that translates self-information into job-seeking terms. The resume introduces you to a potential employer and summarizes what you can offer. A good resume should:

- Accurately portray your background
- Emphasize your strengths
- Be neat, complete, and concise
- Have *no* spelling or grammatical errors

The descriptions you use for internships and/or employment experience should be short and concise—you can even use bullet points—starting with verbs that emphasize the accomplishments and skills you have developed. (The skills you identified in Unit Two will help you with this part.) The headings that you use on the resume should emphasize your strengths and experience (e.g., Internships, Leadership, Involvement).

At the top of the resume it is important to provide cell phone and any other appropriate phone numbers where you can be reached in addition to your e-mail address. The mailing address at the top of the resume should be where you are at the time of the search. Although most employers do not check references until later in the search process, you should obtain references (with e-mail addresses and phone numbers) and be ready to provide them when they are requested.

The most common resume format is the chronological, but the functional resume may be used when there are large gaps in employment. In order to determine which format will best represent your qualifications, consult with your instructor, check the Internet for examples, or review some of the resume publications that can be found in your library or a bookstore.

Chronological Format

The chronological resume is most familiar to employers. In it, jobs are listed in reverse chronological order, beginning with the most recent work experience and including information about the length of your employment, your employer, and the responsibilities and experience you gained on the job. (See Figure A.1.)

The main advantages of the chronological format are its familiarity to employers, the ease with which it can be prepared, and its ability to emphasize a steady work record. Its main disadvantage is its tendency to emphasize gaps in employment or lack of a well-developed employment history.

Functional Format

The functional resume does not emphasize dates and employers, but focuses instead on skills. It generally lists two or three skill areas to reflect the skills you gained in any and all previously held jobs, including any volunteer experiences. (See Figure A.2.)

The main advantages of the functional format are its emphasis on accomplishment and skill areas and its ability to camouflage a spotty or underdeveloped employment record. Its main disadvantage is that its structure may be more difficult to follow. In addition, the potential employer may want to know specifically where and when your identified skills were developed. It is still recommended, therefore, that employment history be included.

Sample Resumes

Now that you know more about how resumes are written, review the examples in Figures A.1 and A.2 more closely. Then look ahead to the resume-writing activities on pages 103–106. Notice that the difference in the two formats is primarily in Section III (Work History).

You can adapt the sections of your resume to suit your particular situation and abilities. In the chronological resume, for example, the job applicant adapted Section IV (Honors) and Section V (Activities and Interests) to focus on his leadership abilities and involvement in the community. In the functional resume, the job applicant provided additional information about her educational background.

Now it's your turn. Choose the format that will present your own experience most favorably and complete the appropriate resume draft activity.

JOHN DOE

Campus Address
2222 Smith Hall
Columbus, OH 43210
(614) 293-0000
jdoe.17@OSU.edu

Permanent Address
482 Cranberry Lane
Berea, OH 44017
(216) 243-4106

CAREER OBJECTIVE: To obtain an internship in accounting.

EDUCATION: **The Ohio State University,** Columbus, Ohio
Bachelor of Science, Business Administration, June 20XX
Major in Accounting, Minor in Economics
Overall GPA: 3.0/4.0

WORK EXPERIENCE: **The Ohio State University,** Columbus, Ohio
(20XX–20XX)
Executive treasurer for a 450-resident dormitory. Prepared
annual budgets, maintained a change fund, and was
responsible for collection and disbursement of all monies.
Implemented a new bookkeeping format, replacing the
old one.

Stevens Management Company, Willoughby, Ohio
(summers of 20XX, 20XX)
Service manager assistant for newly developed condo-
minium project. Responsible for contacting property con-
tractors during construction and for resolving homeowner
service requests as they occurred.

INTERNSHIP: **Daedallan Systems, Inc.,** Cleveland, Ohio
(summers of 20XX–20XX)
Office assistant for independent service bureau. Tasks
included data transmission, printing reports and customer
statements, and preparing statements for mailing.

LEADERSHIP: President, Student Accounting Association
Chair, Homecoming Weekend

INVOLVEMENT: Member, Economics Club, Men's Glee Club
Professional clown performer

REFERENCES: Available upon request.

Figure A.1   Sample Resume (Chronological Approach)

JANE DOE

Current Address
90 Sheldon Avenue
Oswego, NY 13126
(124) 786-1234
jd.408@OSNY.edu

Permanent Address
4240 Kodak Way
Rochester, NY 14623
(222) 871-4321

CAREER OBJECTIVE
To obtain a position in a juvenile court system using my analytical, problem-solving, and research skills.

EDUCATION
State University of New York, Oswego, NY
Bachelor of Arts, Majors in Psychology and Criminology, 20XX
GPA 3.3/4.0
Personally financed 100% of college expenses through employment and scholarships.

COURSE HIGHLIGHTS

Social Psychology	Constitutional Law
Adolescent Psychology	Law and Society
Psychology of Law	Spanish
Research Psychology	Social Work Law

SKILL AREAS
Interviewing
- Advise students on academic, personal, and social matters in a campus residential setting.
- Make appropriate referrals.
- Intern with a school psychologist and share responsibility for counseling/tutoring of high school students experiencing adjustment difficulties.
- Screen and interview candidates being considered for resident adviser positions.

Research
- Assist psychology faculty member with research design to assess and modify social environments.
- Focus on classrooms, residence halls, and union facilities.

EMPLOYMENT HISTORY
- *Researcher,* State University of New York (20XX–present)
- *Intern,* Oswego High School, Oswego, New York (20XX–20XX)
- *Resident Adviser,* State University of New York (20XX–20XX)
- *Server,* Mister Steak, Rochester, New York (summers)

REFERENCES
Available upon request.

Figure A.2   Sample Resume (Functional Approach)

ACTIVITY A.1 RESUME—FIRST DRAFT
(CHRONOLOGICAL APPROACH)

Name: _____

Campus address (effective dates): _____   Permanent address: _____

_____   _____

_____   _____

Cell phone: _____   Telephone: _____

E-mail: _____

I. Job Objective (or capsule resume)

In addition to naming the type of work you are seeking, try condensing your qualifications in a short statement at the start of your resume. For example: "Initial position in some phase of environmental control research. Have laboratory skills. VISTA volunteer for three summers." or "Management trainee position in the banking industry involving supervisory and planning skills. Long-range goal is branch management."

_____

_____

_____

_____

_____

II. Education

Condense your educational qualifications here. Always put the most recent first.

_____

_____

_____

_____

_____

_____

_____

(continued)

III. Work History

List each of your jobs, with the most recent first. Give dates of employment to account for all of your time, names of employers, titles of positions, and duties you performed in detail. Mention specific achievements in each job. Quantify if possible (e.g., "supervised 10 staff members").

Dates	Employers	Position Title and Duties

IV. Honors

List any honors you have received or any honors activities in which you have been involved.

_____

_____

_____

_____

V. Activities and Interests

Highlight your professional and personal interests that would be of most interest to an employer.

_____

_____

_____

_____

VI. References

Write a statement that references are available upon request, or list the names, addresses, phone numbers, and e-mail addresses of two or three references that the employer can contact directly.

_____

_____

_____

_____

ACTIVITY A.2: RESUME—FIRST DRAFT
(FUNCTIONAL APPROACH)

Name: _____

Campus address (effective dates): _____   Permanent address: _____

_____   _____

_____   _____

Cell phone: _____   Telephone: _____

E-mail: _____

I. Job Objective (or capsule resume)

In addition to naming the type of work you are seeking, try condensing your qualifications in a short statement at the start of your resume. For example: "Initial position in some phase of environmental control research. Have laboratory skills. VISTA volunteer for three summers." or "Management trainee position in the banking industry involving supervisory and planning skills. Long-range goal is branch management."

_____

_____

_____

_____

_____

_____

II. Education

Condense your educational qualifications here. Always put the most recent first.

_____

_____

_____

_____

_____

_____

_____

(*continued*)

III. Work History

List the skills and abilities you have developed or demonstrated. You do not need to associate one skill with one employer; you may have used one skill in several jobs.

Skills or Abilities	Job Titles and Responsibilities	Employers and Dates
_____	_____	_____
_____	_____	_____
_____	_____	_____
_____	_____	_____

IV. Honors

List any honors you have received or any honors activities in which you have been involved.

_____

_____

_____

V. Activities and Interests

Highlight your professional and personal interests that would be of most interest to an employer.

_____

_____

_____

_____

VI. References

Write a statement that references are available upon request, or list the names, addresses, phone numbers, and e-mail addresses of two or three references that the employer can contact directly. (It is often recommended that this list be on a separate sheet.)

_____

_____

_____

_____

COVER LETTERS

When you apply for a position—especially if you are doing so online—you should submit a cover letter along with your resume. The *cover letter* can provide information that is generally not included in the resume, and it also personalizes your application.

The first paragraph usually identifies the position for which you are applying, may indicate where you heard about the position, and tells why you are interested in this particular position.

The second paragraph can add information about yourself that directly pertains to the specific position and reinforces important items in the resume itself. For example, you could briefly describe successful and relevant experiences that would benefit the prospective employer.

The last paragraph in a cover letter usually provides a phone number or an e-mail address where you can be reached and may inform the reader that you will be in contact to arrange a possible interview.

Cover letters are an important part of the job search process. Retain a copy of each letter in an organized job search file. A good cover letter and a well-developed resume are invaluable when your goal is to elicit a response that will lead to an interview. Figure A.3 is an example of a cover letter.

90 Sheldon Avenue
Oswego, NY 13126

March 1, 20XX

James A. Smith
Oswego County Juvenile Court
70 Spring Street
Oswego, NY 13111

Dear Mr. Smith:

My major professor at the State University of New York in Oswego, Dr. Lew Burns, has informed me of your recently posted position in the Juvenile Court system. As you can see from my enclosed resume, I will receive a degree in psychology and criminology in June. I am extremely interested in your position, and as a result of my education and experiences, I feel I bring strong qualifications for your consideration.

I have been involved in many paid and volunteer activities that have prepared me for work in the juvenile system. I interned with a public school psychologist during my junior and senior years and spent many hours in juvenile court working with offenders and observing how the system works. I have individually counseled several troubled youths and feel I had a positive impact on them. I also have strong research skills, having worked on several funded projects involving the etiology and behavior of juvenile offenders.

I would appreciate an opportunity to speak with you about the tasks involved in the position and to inform you in more detail about my expertise and qualifications. I will call you the week of March 4 to possibly set up an appointment. If you wish to reach me before then, please contact me at 444-6789 or jd.408@OSNY.edu. Thank you for considering me for an interview.

Sincerely,

Jane Doe

Jane Doe

Figure A.3   Sample Cover Letter

INTERVIEW PREPARATION

Your careful preparation for interviews with recruiters or representatives from potential employers is extremely important. Job fairs or career days on your campus usually serve as a first screening. If you are well prepared for this first screening you will tremendously enhance your chances of being called for a second interview, usually held at the recruiter's offices.

You will want to learn as much as possible about the organization before interviewing with them. You should try to anticipate some of the questions you will be asked and have questions of your own prepared. The interviewer will be impressed if you can show that you have "done your homework" on the company and are able to ask intelligent questions about working there. This cannot be emphasized enough.

Your campus career services office should have information about organizations that conduct on-campus interviews. The most current information, however, can be found on the organization's Web site. And most important, remember to read and learn any materials you received from the interviewer at your first interview.

Large companies that do a lot of entry-level hiring often use behavioral-based interviews. These questions ask students to give an example of a specific situation in which they have used a certain skill or exhibited a particular quality. Some examples include the following:

- Tell me about a time you analyzed data and made a recommendation.
- Tell me about a time when you failed.
- Give me an example of a time you had a conflict with a coworker and tell me how you resolved it.
- Give me an example of a time you effectively solved a problem.

When responding to a question, always talk through the *situation,* the *action* you took, and the *result.* It takes practice to answer these types of questions effectively. Preparation is key to effective interviewing. Employers want to see enthusiasm from the interviewee for their organization and why they would be a good fit.

After the interview it is essential that you make a phone call to thank the interviewer for his or her time and add any other information that was not covered in the interview. If you cannot reach the interviewer, leave a message. It is also important to send a brief thank-you e-mail or text message so that you can express your thanks for the interview and repeat your interest in the position. Because many students do not follow up in this way, it might help to separate you from your competition.